State-Owned Enterprises in a Mixed Economy

State-Owned Enterprises in a Mixed Economy

Micro Versus Macro Economic Objectives

Mehdi Haririan

Routledge
Taylor & Francis Group
LONDON AND NEW YORK

First published 1989 by Westview Press, Inc.

Published 2019 by Routledge
52 Vanderbilt Avenue, New York, NY 10017
2 Park Square, Milton Park, Abingdon, Oxon OX14 4RN

Routledge is an imprint of the Taylor & Francis Group, an informa business

Library of Congress Cataloging-in-Publication Data
Haririan, Mehdi
State-owned enterprises in a mixed economy: micro versus macro economic objectives
p. cm.—(Westview special studies in industrial policy and development)
Includes index.
ISBN 0-8133-7699-8
1. Government business enterprises. 2. Efficiency, Industrial. I. Title. II. Series.
HD3850.H36 1989
350.009'2—dc19 **88-36479**
CIP

ISBN 13: 978-0-367-28877-8 (hbk)

ISBN 13: 978-0-367-30423-2 (pbk)

To my father, Mohamad Rahim Haririan,
and my mother, Maryam Ronasi,
who helped me to appreciate the importance
of scholarship and ideas

and to my wife, Christine,
for her understanding and moral support
during the preparation of this book

Contents

Tables and Figures

Appendices

Foreword

Recently, a large number of books have been published praising the efficiency of market processes and demonstrating failures of the nonmarket activities of the government sectors. In addition, in the last decade or more, economic programs have been implemented to reduce the government sector and to privatize public firms. State-owned firms, so it is argued, represent failures in allocation of scarce resources, are highly indebted, add to inflation rates, reduce private incentives, and retard economic growth. It is now the dominant view that competitive markets are more efficient and can do better in allocating resources than public, nonmarket forces. Though there is a long tradition in economic theory that spells out that there are failures to be observed for market as well as nonmarket processes, the academic view has become quite one-sided. For the most part, it stresses only that nonmarket, government operations fail.

It is time for a more skeptical view on this academic trend, and one is urged to reflect again on: (1) why markets fail, (2) why, in most countries, such a large government sector exists (in developed as well as developing countries), and (3) what constitutes appropriate performance measures for the public sector and public firms. This book takes a very comprehensive and refreshing view on these matters.

Since the time of Adam Smith's writings on the *Wealth of Nations* , it has also become standard academic knowledge that markets fail. Classical economics gave numerous examples where markets do not operate appropriately. Neoclassical theory claimed to have developed a more rigorous theory of market failures that has become the foundation of public economics in the postwar period. The thorough demonstration of the existence of market failures was an early by-product of general equilibrium theory. The theory of market failures was viewed as the other side of the coin of a perfectly competitive economy, according to which markets are perfectly competitive and efficient if: the agents behave rationally and exhibit maximizing behavior; their decisions are made independently of each other; there are no increasing returns to scale, no collusion, no external effects, and perfect mobility of resources; the number of agents is infinitely large, such that there is no influence on the quantities sold or bought (price-takers); agents' decisions are based on perfect information; and complete future markets exist. Deviations from these strong requirements indicate imperfections and market failures and demand state interventions. The theory of perfectly competitive markets--with the additional assumption of at least local stability properties of the law of supply and demand--became the benchmark for public economics in the postwar period. So it was then easy to measure the performance of the public sector and public firms with the yardstick of a perfectly competitive economy.

However, as the theory progressed, it had also become clear that there are almost no markets to be found where those ideal conditions exist. By now, one realizes that these requirements are theory-generated--to make the theory consistent--but that they have no counterpart in reality. Nevertheless, in a vast part of economic literature, the failures of nonmarket operations are usually measured against perfectly working market processes. Therefore, there is some irony in the historical development of economic theory: the more the theory stresses that its conditions do not correspond to reality, the more the ideal conditions of the theory have become the standards for judging the efficiency of nonmarket processes--an unfortunate development for the public sector and public firms that became the first victims of wrong benchmarks. As persuasively demonstrated in this book, microeconomic efficiency criteria alone, stemming from the theory of a perfectly competitive economy, are badly designed criteria for public firms.

The historical part of the book, in particular, discusses quite compellingly a number of causes other than market failures for the existence of state-owned enterprises. This discussion develops complex answers regarding causes for the existence of public firms. State-owned enterprises have to fulfill a multiplicity of goals, micro as well as macro objectives, and they arose due to a multiplicity of causes, such as: large-scale capital requirements for production, risky ventures, increased economic control of the private sector, balancing uneven development, stimulation of technical change and growth, mitigation of the unemployment problem, changing income distribution, seeking rents and royalties from economic activities, and controlling the socioeconomic development through nationalization and planning. This book gives a comprehensive treatment for the multiple causes of the existence of state-owned enterprises.

Moreover, as convincingly demonstrated, the state-owned enterprises are characterized by contradictory sets of goals: microeconomic efficiency goals, as measured by financial ratios, and macroeconomic objectives, usually not measured or measurable. The book takes this multiplicity of complex and vague goals seriously, departing from the common view that state-owned enterprises should be measured solely by microeconomic efficiency criteria and financial performance ratios.

This leads to the basic innovative idea of the book. Its essential point is that the wide range of disparate--and partly exclusive--objectives does not easily allow a quantitatively oriented performance evaluation of state-owned enterprises. The discussion of this problem is based on extensive material and data, monographs of public firms of different countries, national income account data sets, IMF data series, and empirical studies of other authors. The lack of consistent data sources, particularly on developing countries, makes an empirical appraisal of the performance of state-owned enterprises difficult. The material presented here in support of the view pursued is, nevertheless, quite compelling.

A critical evaluation of the arguments against the state-owned enterprises and their investment criteria, financing practices, and pricing procedures still leaves open the question of how to judge the attainment of public firms' micro- as well as macroeconomic goals. In the book, this question is answered in a new manner. A framework is proposed for evaluating efficiency, investment, financing, and pricing of state-owned enterprises with multiple and contradictory goals. Going beyond the well-known criticism of marginal cost pricing for state-owned firms, the book designs a pricing procedure by utilizing recent advances in the theory of joint production. Pricing procedures for joint production, known from multiplant and multiproduct corporations, appropriately modified, allow us to simultaneously account for micro as well as macro objectives of the public firm. The proposed methods also concur with an integrated treatment of pricing and of investment and financing problems. The proposed new concept of pricing, investment, and financing, as well as performance evaluation of goals of state-owned firms, is notably original and will hopefully initiate further productive discussions.

In sum, this book represents a considerable academic achievement in its serious and constructive treatment of the public sector and state-owned enterprises. The book should become an important work of reference for further research and economic policy.

Willi Semmler

Preface

A distinctive feature of economic trends of the past three decades has been the increase in microeconomic intervention by state-owned enterprises (SOEs) in the market economies of rich industrial and poor developing nations. The majority of SOEs were established as policy instruments of choice in response to a variety of socioeconomic needs and sociopolitical problems. Since SOEs by nature have complex multiple objectives, conflicts often arise and trade-offs may be necessary. Performance evaluations of such enterprises should be based on their success in meeting their predetermined targets, i.e., Goal Attainment Model. Social objectives place a cost burden on SOEs and adversely affect their financial viability. After the costs of these noncommercial objectives (NCOs) have been evaluated, the government compensation of SOEs should be based on Reversing the Burden of Proof Principle. This principle, in conjunction with cost-plus pricing rather than marginal costs pricing, will provide greater accuracy in projecting financial needs.

The involvement of SOEs in capital-intensive industries that have capital requirements that are both risky and lumpy may require some dependency on the public treasury or the acceptance of inferior rates of return as compared to their private counterparts in order to achieve social optimality. In spite of this fact, privatization as a policy option has been adopted by a number of industrial nations. This policy, which stems from the belief that privatization will remedy the inherent and ostensibly inefficient performance of SOEs, ignores the fact that their creation was based on different motives and their continuing existence should be based on their effectiveness in achieving social and national objectives. Profitability is a biased and incomplete indicator of performance. Furthermore, even when the specific characteristics of SOEs require massive subsidization, such subsidies are usually only a small part of the overall budget. Thus, SOEs should not be blamed for the burgeoning deficits of central governments. The privatization strategy currently followed by industrialized nations is neither transferable nor practical for use in the developing nations. This book proposes some answers in regard to the equivocal position of supporters of privatization.

Mehdi Haririan
Bloomsburg University
of Pennsylvania

1

Growth and Expansion of SOEs

This chapter will concentrate on the causes of growth and expansion of state-owned enterprises (SOEs). SOEs will be studied from their political, historical, and economic perspectives. Some of the factors that prevent the derivation of more rigorous theoretical models concerning the behavior of SOEs will be discussed, and the reasons for expansion of mixed enterprises will also be investigated. One of the main characteristics of SOEs, capital intensity, will be discussed here, but the results of empirical studies, including those by the author, will be deferred until Chapters 2 and 4.

Expansion and growth of public enterprises, particularly SOEs, in the developed and developing countries has occurred for different economic and noneconomic reasons. A proper classification of the motives and causes goes a long way toward a meaningful understanding of the social evolution of the behavior of the SOEs. Therefore, the motives and causes of the growth and expansion of SOEs will be summarized in this chapter, and the economic effect of the SOEs resulting from their pricing, investment, and employment policies will be analyzed in other chapters.

Causes and Motives

The reasons and motives for governments to run a particular sector or industry differ from sector to sector or industry to industry. These reasons sometimes overlap, and, therefore, a clear-cut distinction for discussing a single cause is almost impossible. Also, these causes and motives cannot be discussed independent of time. Taking the time factor into consideration and putting the SOEs in a dynamic framework makes the analysis and study of the causes and motives for running an enterprise by the state more appropriate. For example, transfer of power from a conservative to a labor government in the U.K. would change the government's motive for running a sector by the state into an incentive for expansion that encompasses other sectors. Before we look at the causes and motives for expansion of SOEs, it is necessary to emphasize that SOEs and private enterprises look different when seen from different perspectives. Multiplicity of objectives and confusing, contradictory, unquantified, and vague objectives are only a part of the problem. Problems of contradiction are intensified when there are conflicts of interest among different organs of the government. For example, the ministry of industry and the ministry of finance could well have conflicting objectives. The former may be in favor of encouraging more investment and the latter in favor of restricting and discouraging more expenditure by the SOE. So there are two kinds of conflicts and multiplicity. One involves the objectives of an SOE itself and the other a conflict among the controllers.

Generalized, ambiguous, and vague objectives are characteristic of most SOEs in different countries. For example, national interest is a generalized and vague objective without any precise and measurable parameters. The following examples of stated contradictory and multiple objectives of SOEs in the U.K. illustrate this point:

> ...to promote the efficient and economic supply of iron and steel products in such quantities and at such prices as may seem to them best calculated to meet the reasonable demands of customers and to further the public's interest (Treasury 1976, Paragraph 30).

> ...making supplies of coal available of such qualities and sizes and in such quantities and at such prices, as may seem to them best calculated to further the public interest in all respects, including the avoidance of any undue or unreasonable preference or advantage (Treasury 1946, Section 1).

Most of the objectives of SOEs are derived from public policy geared toward the achievement of some national goals and public interest. However, these goals, as noted above, are stated in rather general terms and cannot be stated in quantifiable dimensions. Qualitative characteristics of national interest create conflict among different sponsor organizations that somehow have their responsibility related to the activities of SOEs. In other words, arguing the national interest in a general form is not problematic; the real problem is the difficulty of translating the general and extremely nebulous statement into precise and quantitative figures. It is here that the main distinction between a private enterprise and an SOE becomes more apparent. In this context, the problem is further intensified by the multiple objectives of SOEs that reflect political pressures and conflicting national interests. The issue of national interest creates a big difference between private enterprises and SOEs when seen from different perspectives, such as managerial discretion. In the case of private enterprise, the managerial discretion can be stated in terms of divergence from a single objective, such as profit maximization. But such simplification cannot be made for the SOEs not only because of multiplicity of objectives but also because of the contradictory and conflicting nature of objectives.

The difference between private enterprises and SOEs is not limited to managerial discretion only. Peltzman (1989, 73) argues that "there is no simple dichotomy between SOEs and privately owned firms with respect to the behavior we can expect from them." The conditions in which an SOE operates are very different from those of a private enterprise. SOEs operate outside market forces, but private enterprises operate within market forces. The survival and growth of any dynamic private enterprises depend on the proper use of their funds. Misuse of funds and involvement in risky investments would threaten their survival and may ultimately lead to bankruptcy. For this reason, managers of private enterprises are conservative and cautious about the outcome of investments. In the case of SOEs, the link between survival and efficient use of finances is missing, and the consequent lack of punishment by market forces not only causes less attention to be paid to the question of efficiency but also frees managers to pay more attention to the expansion of the SOE. This issue is related to whether or not the SOE is a tool for carrying out public policies.

The degree of pressure and power of outsiders and insiders in the activities of the two kinds of enterprises is different. In the case of private enterprises, because of the profit maximization objective, the search for primary and intermediate inputs at lowest costs is an important dynamic process. For the SOE , such an option is much less important. Pressure on the SOE to choose a domestic supplier over a foreign one and to purchase inputs from other SOEs invariably results in an increase in its costs of production. However, the implicit objectives emerging from such pressure could very well be the result of other macro and social objectives, e.g., employment creation. Labor unions in SOEs are generally stronger than in private enterprises, and, as a result of this political power, they not only demand higher money wages but also ask for more social wages and greater job security. Their wages and salaries might even be viewed as a fixed cost for an SOE because, even in times of recession, redundant workers cannot be dismissed. With their greater job security, the unions are often able to increase their political clout and obtain even more concessions during collective bargaining (Kendall 1972, Chapter 10).

People in charge of running private enterprises, as long as they follow the objective of profit maximization, have the option of choosing their strategy. In the case of SOEs, such an option is circumscribed by other social objectives and by politicians behavior. Consequently, these differences in the objectives of the two kinds of enterprises lead to entirely different kinds of constraints in the choice of strategies. Private enterprises often adopt the concept of diversification for their organization's growth and survival. The adoption of such measures ensures the effective use of resources by transferring them from declining and losing sectors to more profitable ones. Restrictions that are imposed on SOEs by considerations such as domestic legislation or even international treaties and by social pressure from private sectors prevent the SOEs from adopting similar strategies. However, the concept of diversification and mobility of resources is not unrelated to social objectives. If the government transfers resources out of the sectors that are presently run by the government, e.g., British Rail, or halts new investment for replacement, the result could be a decline in the scale of operation and/or the quality of their services. The government should enter into new industries and the surpluses generated could be used to subsidize those declining industries that may have important social objectives. The question is: What is the position of private sectors in this regard, and are the SOEs welcome to compete with them?

Economic Reasons

First of all, it is important to recognize that classification of motives and causes is arbitrary, and there is overlap between and within them. The weight that may be assigned to each economic cause in different countries depends on the stage of development and growth of each country. We shall attempt to pinpoint the main economic causes.

Most of the industries that need large amounts of fixed capital or a high ratio of fixed capital to variable costs are concentrated under government ownership (Lintner 1981, 23). The reasons for such a trend in developed and developing countries may be different, but regardless of the reasons and circumstances, it is an established fact (Pryor, 1973, Chapter 2 passim). We notice a great deal of state investment in industries such as telecommunications, transportation, utilities, steel, refineries, etc., with little or no investment in industries such as textiles, forestry, chemicals, and rubber. The large investment by government in some industries is not usually based on the expected economic return but is often based on other reasons, such as the desire to control key industries and prevent the concentration of power in private hands. For example, the "Second Industrial Policy Resolution" of India imposed barriers to entry of commercial companies in twenty-nine industries.

In some countries, SOEs have invested in highly capital-intensive industries as a means of import substitution. The involvement of SOEs in such industries is usually intended to make the country industrially independent of other countries. In some nations, SOEs are in capital-intensive industries because of entrepreneurial substitution by the state. This is the case with industries such as steel in Korea and Argentina. This development takes place because of the inability and/or unwillingness of private entrepreneurs to invest in such enterprises. Their reluctance may be due to the size of projects or the risk and uncertainty involved. This is usually the case in developing countries like Turkey and Pakistan.

Still another reason may be to prevent the widening of a technological gap or to achieve a higher level of technology. This is one reason that state intervention and investment increased in some of the European countries. They were concerned about the widening of the technological gap between Europe and the United States that could place their domestic industries in a weaker competitive position and/or place them under the control of international companies. For example, in Italy, as Holland (1974, 34) has pointed out, investment in highly modern food processing SOEs is the result of a fear that U.S. firms would dominate Italian food processing companies. Again, in such cases the underlying reasons for state control play a more important role than the return on investment. Thus, expansion of state participation is a reaction to the growth of foreign and domestic private enterprises in some industries. Vernon (1974, 19) believes that the "persistent nationalization in high technology industries has been exacerbated when the participants were state-owned enterprises."

Linkage and Interdependency (Externalities)

Linkage and interdependency are closely related to the state of capital intensity discussed above. Estimates of private benefits may be biased and may underestimate the full potential influence of public enterprise. When implicit yield from externalities is excluded, the financial returns inevitably result in an underestimate of the true yield. If similar investment criteria were adopted for investment decisions by public enterprises, the result would be the possible rejection of many investments. The adoption of criteria that fail to take into account the full direct and indirect impact of investment on the rest of the economy will discourage investment.

Most SOEs have high forward and backward linkage effects or externalities. This factor of externalities is one of the main reasons for governments to undertake industrial enterprises, even when some of them do not show any surpluses. A full contribution of such sectors could be calculated only when their role in stimulating other economic activities is considered. In other words, we should try to find out what the influence of an industry or a particular sector on the growth of the economy is, and, if such calculations are possible, the sector under consideration should have a multiplier effect on the growth of the economy. One of the tools that could enhance such an understanding and also provide some proxy measure of the role of a particular sector in the economy is the so-called "Hirschmanian Concept" of linkages. This concept is a helpful tool and should be used for individual industry case studies or for the study of the economy in a wider perspective by using input-output tables. One of the problems with this approach, however, is that when an input-output table is used for measuring these linkages, the result is likely to be distorted by double counting. Hirschman was aware of the problem, and he called his effort a "mental experiment" (Hirschman , quoted in Jones 1975, 98).

Monopoly

Neoclassical general equilibrium theory prescribes the conditions and assumptions under which competitive market economy leads to Pareto efficiency. When these assumptions are violated, intervention by the government results in a socially superior condition as compared to a free market economy. One such violation is the existence of monopoly that results in a distortion of efficient resource allocation. If the government is concerned about such distortions, it must step in. There are different policy options available to deal with this kind of market failure. These policies could be in the form of either limited or full intervention. The limited intervention includes policies concerning competition, regulation, and taxation. If such limited intervention does not create sufficient control, then the only solution to the problem of allocative inefficiency is full intervention in the form of public production. In some cases, there is no policy option except public ownership and control, especially when the constitution of a country is explicitly antimonopoly. These cases are not rare and can be found in the constitutions of countries such as Germany, England, Belgium, France, and Italy.

One reason for opposition to the existence of monopolies in some industries or production entities is to prevent the negative effect of such market imperfections on the rest of the economy. Some of the other reasons for proscribing monopolies include the national interest, the prevention of the concentration of economic power resulting from economies of scale, and economic rent that is earned from such economies of scale that may, in turn, have a negative effect on the distribution of income. Monopolies restrict output and set the prices based on their elasticity of demand and income constraints of consumers. Invariably, their prices are higher than those in competitive markets. Furthermore, monopolies tend to change income distribution in favor of monopolists. To the extent effective demand is a function of the distribution of income, the distribution of products, too, becomes lopsided in favor of the richer classes. Thus, monopolies distort resource allocation, product-mix, volume of output, and the distribution of products. All these make an excellent case for public intervention to prevent the growth of private monopolies.

Micro/Macroeconomic Motives

The objectives of SOEs may be classified in several ways: microeconomic, macroeconomic, short-term, long-term, commercial, non-commercial, primary, and secondary. All of these objectives can be achieved by different means and policies, but one thing that is common among these diverse objectives is that, depending on the size and market share of SOEs, they could influence the financial markets and result in a conflict with the original objectives set for the SOEs.

Assume, for a moment, regardless of the kind of classification, that the purposes and objectives are unique and include national policy, commercial objectives, efficiency, and a better distribution of incomes. When SOEs are used as instruments of national policy, these national goals will often conflict with commercial objectives. For example, fighting inflation seldom creates employment; efficient cost minimization often involves the discharge of surplus labor. Feasibility studies are often conducted before making investment decisions in the private sector and usually consider areas involving technology, engineering, and managerial decisions. They do not consider job creation, income disparities between regions, or the overall distribution of income. From a purely technological viewpoint, a single large-scale plant might be the most efficient project, but social objectives might favor the use of a number of smaller, less efficient plants. Thus, one of the main reasons for locating industries in the southern part of Italy and the northern part of Sweden was the creation of jobs and equality of income distribution in different parts of these countries. If the government uses SOEs as a means of achieving macroeconomic goals and disregards the question of efficient allocation of resources, in the long run its operation would work against these goals.

From the perspective of some welfare economists, such as Pigou, Bergson, and Lerner, when there is a market failure, intervention by the government is considered superior to the performance of the free market. However, SOEs in different countries have been creatures of not only this contingency but of many different circumstances, and the same enterprises in different countries may not have the same origin.

We have thus far examined some of the reasons for setting up SOEs and have discussed their objectives, which may vary from the rescue of ailing private enterprises to the establishment of totally new enterprises to promote economic development. SOEs are often used as tools for dynamic development by creating import substitutes and promoting exports. For example, in Italy during the 1950s, SOEs accepted the responsibility of bringing about industrial change by providing a new technostructure for such a goal (Prodi 1974, 50). In the early 1960s, both the Italian Institute for Industrial Reconstruction (IRI) and State Hydrocarbons Corporation (ENI) had national support as instruments of modernization and balanced growth (Martinelli 1981, 91). The existence of SOEs can improve the functioning of domestic markets and prevent encroachment by foreign multinational corporations.

Whenever risk and uncertainty retard private investment, SOEs become necessary, and they can more easily meet the large capital requirements of modern technology. National planners use SOEs to provide the necessary linkages among interdependent private enterprises. The SOEs affect the distribution and allocation of resources and provide long-term benefits for the entire economy. They may provide stable economic growth during the downswing of the business cycle when private enterprises are contracting. In some cases, SOEs may even serve as a source of revenue for the government. The Norwegian and British governments, for example, believe that the state ownership of oil companies will not only increase the national income but also help promote a greater understanding of the international oil market (Krapels 1977, 32). However, the maximization of financial returns will conflict with social objectives. Therefore, it is important to clarify which goals a given SOE will be expected to attain.

SOEs from a Historical Perspective

From a historical perspective, SOEs are not a new phenomenon. They have a long history and ancient origin. For instance, minting coinage is not a new area of coverage by the state. This and other similar areas that have been operated by the state for centuries are called an "old generation" of SOEs. The "new generation," in economic activities, is the result of historical forces and the sociopolitical needs of capitalist societies for survival. The recurrence of economic crises in such societies further spurred government involvement. In Italy, for instance, the economic crisis of the 1930s promoted and enhanced the intervention of the state in the economy. IRI was created in 1933 for the protection and security of major industries in Italy. Mussolini referred to the IRI as a clinic for rescuing firms that were temporarily in trouble (Mussolini, quoted in Martinelli 1981, 88). *Gestionie Partecipazione Industriale* was created in 1976 to help some industries adjust to pressure from trade unions and politicians, a step subsequently called a "rescue operation, Italian style" (Prodi 1974, 50).

In France, too, state intervention has been the result of special circumstances and crises (Michalet 1974, 109). For example, Renault was taken over after World War II mainly because the owners collaborated with the occupying power (the Nazis). Some enterprises, such as France's *Compagnie Generale Transatlantique,* were taken over by the government because they ran into financial crises. The Depression of the 1930s was another reason why the government of France took over such industries as coal, gas, electricity, and principal banks and insurance companies. Similarly, in Austria, Korea, and Taiwan, state intervention and nationalization followed from special circumstances (Walstedt 1980, 17). Thus, the Korean government took over industries such as railroads and communications that belonged to the colonial regime and others such as electricity and banking, that belonged to private Japanese owners (Jones 1975, 131). In Sweden, financial crises and private sector bankruptcies resulted in either state intervention or, in some cases, the actual takeover of such industries as shipbuilding, textiles, steel, and forestry. In the U.K., some industries were taken over by the government as a matter of inevitability (Keyser, Windle, and Stares 1978, 12). British Leyland, for example, was taken over by the conservative British government because of its role in employment and export. The U.K., after World War II, accelerated the pace of acquiring industries such as coal and gas. Historically, large-scale failure of private enterprises in the shipbuilding and aerospace sectors is another reason for the increased takeover of industries in the U.K.

SOEs from a Political Perspective

The creation, establishment, and expansion of SOEs is sometimes seen as strongly related to political purposes. The specific nature of these purposes or objectives may vary from country to country and from time to time within the same country, depending upon their internal and external political-economic circumstances and upon the stage of their socioeconomic development. For example, the originally stated objective of industrialization at the time of establishing IRI and ENI changed over time to an instrument of political control of industry. In some countries, the political purposes for controlling and owning enterprises are so strong that the use of any economic standards for measuring their performance is considered irrelevant. Many of the industries in developing countries are based on political objectives, not economic ones. Some lessons can, indeed, be learned from those nations that have a long history of SOEs. It may be useful for developing countries to realize that the long-run survival of SOEs, if based entirely on political considerations in complete disregard of their economic and financial viability, is almost impossible. Depending on the size, share, and continuation of an SOE's deficit, the government might either introduce financial viability criteria or transfer the ownership of losing enterprises to the private sector. The first alternative was used by France and England, and the latter has been used by Sweden.

In some cases, the state took over industrial enterprises in order to improve industrial relations by having more worker participation in decisionmaking and by providing better pay and working conditions. Renault, a state-owned car producer in France, is the most progressive employer and pays the best wages in the country (Kessler 1978). Another political objective is to prevent the control of "commanding height industries" by the private sector, which is a deliberately designed political strategy to transfer power to the state. This, in turn, is intended to make income distribution more equal. In other words, democratic rather than market control of industries is perceived to improve income distribution since the profit goes to the public. SOEs are often used as tools for implementing other government policies, such as curbing inflation and creating jobs. The extent to which these political objectives can be achieved depends upon the strength of the party in power.

SOEs may be seen as political instruments designed to safeguard both present and future socioeconomic well-being. In the late 1960s and early 1970s in Europe, many SOEs were established to counterbalance growing multinational enterprises (Holland 1974, 34). In many developed and developing countries, SOEs emerged as a counterbalance to the concentration of private domestic producers, as in Korea, or large oligopolies, as in the case of ENI in Italy. In summary, as pointed out by Sheahan (1976b, 215), the expansion or establishment of SOEs is often based on political rather than economic objectives, especially in developing countries. However, as noted earlier, political aims usually change over time, and there is a tendency toward control and party management of the economy. Political objectives include the creation of employment and the improvement of industrial relations. The existence of multinational corporations or giant domestic oligopolies often interferes with the attainment of these objectives. The formation of SOEs is designed to counterbalance this interference.

SOEs Defined

The touchy question of defining an SOE has been delayed until we have fully explored the causes and motives for the existence of such enterprises. A review of literature on this subject provides us with a wide variety of definitions, each based on the purposes, forms, economic expectations, and legal and organizational structures of various countries. The concepts of private and public are not without confusion either because what is public in one country could be private in another. This lack of homogeneity prevents us from adopting a single definition to cover all situations. Public enterprise could be defined, based on its objectives, as narrowly as possible or as broadly as we wish.

The problem of defining an SOE is further confounded by the fact that only in a small number of Organization for Economic Cooperation and Development (OECD) countries are SOEs treated separately in the national accounts. A few countries, such as France and the U.K., provide a list of the public enterprises in their national accounts, but they do not offer any rationale as to why they have classified them as such. Furthermore, the number of enterprises classified as private in one country could change dramatically if we adopted the classification criteria of some other country. In other words, private and public classification differs from country to country, depending upon the political and institutional framework of each. Also, it is important to realize that ownership and control may rest in different parties in different countries, depending upon their particular legislation and regulation. The lack of data and information are further constraints on any international comparison of SOEs as a package. In view of these difficulties, we were obliged to narrow our perspective to a very specific type of public enterprise.

In defining a public enterpise, each author has emphasized his own area of interest. In this book, we are primarily interested in the economic aspects of SOEs, so those elements that have more economic implications have been chosen in our attempt to coin our own definition of an SOE. In reviewing the literature related to public enterprise, we find there are some aspects that are common to various definitions, but the weights assigned by different authors to each element are different. The main elements are ownership, degree of government control, marketability, sales, autonomy of management, and the portion of costs covered by sales. We find these elements common in the definitions provided by Johansen (1965, 187), United Nations (1968, 78), Hanson (1968, 1), Wickham (1969, 326), Houssiaux (1969, 424), Organization for Economic Cooperation and Development (1981, 5), Lintner (1981, 33), World Bank (1983, 48), Shirley (1983, 2), Floyd (1983, 1), Short (1983, 2), Aharoni (1986, 6), International Monetary Fund (1986, 20), and Ramamurti (1987, 3). From the definitions, we note that the coverage and boundary specifications are vague, arbitrary, and irrational. For example, a classification based on ownership is unclear because it leaves out questions on what percentage of the equity shares should belong to the state. Also, in considering this basis of classification, the inclusion or exclusion of subsidiaries of SOEs is highly relevant. The exclusion of subsidiaries may result in underestimating the true magnitude of the public enterprise sector for those countries that have a significant equity share in subsidiaries, e.g., Italy. Basically, we shall use the definitions given by others, but with our own modifications. Each SOE could be defined differently based upon its objectives. In other words, if SOEs operated on the same principles as private enterprises and had only commercial objectives, then they should be defined on the basis of economic model and criteria. If SOEs have both commercial objectives and NCOs, then using a purely economic model for evaluating overall performance would be misleading, and adjustments in the definition for deviation from the economic model need to be made.

SOEs are defined on the basis of such common elements as ownership, control, marketedness, autonomy and freedom, objectives and motives, self-financing ratios, and explicit and implicit subsidies. They are productive entities that produce goods and services that are not only marketable but also marketed. Thus, the exclusion principle may be applied. They are owned and controlled by the government, and their self-financing ratios are dependent upon constraints preset by the government for economic variables and NCOs. The magnitude of their subsidies, either implicit or explicit, is identifiable.

Economic Theory and Firm Behavior

The application of pure economic theory to understand the behavior of an SOE is problematic. Some scholars, such as Lerner (1944) and Lange and Taylor (1938), have attempted to derive a theory of economic behavior for the SOEs. However, as pointed out by Baumol (1965, 63), their theories suffer from major defects:

> It is surprising that in Professor Lerner's book on the economic theory of government control there is no mention of external economies anywhere in more than five hundred pages, inasmuch as this serves to eliminate much of the ground for a critical examination of the status quo. It is hardly astounding, then, that Lerner comes to the conclusion that the characteristics of perfect competition constitute a satisfactory norm for the proper organization and conduct of a socialist economy.

Explaining the expansion and growth of SOEs in the twentieth century in terms of political theory rather than economic theory provides a more realistic set of ideas, even from the point of view of orthodox economists such as Vernon and Aharoni (1981, 7) and Bös (1981, 123). In order to arrive at a better economic theory of SOEs, theories of the socialist economy to explain the growth and behavior of SOEs were advanced by economists such as Lange. However, the end-product of his investigation was a return to the classical theory of economics that postulates that the government prevents the private sector from gaining monopolistic power, rather than the development of a new theory of economics (Vernon and Aharoni 1981, 9-10). Pryor (1973, 351) viewed Lange's model as "merely a bureaucratic market surrogate." Most of the SOEs in the capitalist countries do not have monopoly characteristics, and they coexist in harmony with private enterprises. Therefore, it may be more appropriate to consider the SOEs in an oligopolistic model rather than in monopolistic or perfectly competitive models. In other words, we suggest that the expansion of SOEs should be studied within the framework of a mixed economy.

We may next consider the near impossibility of deriving a theory for SOEs. Some economists, such as Raiffa (1981, 56), Cassese (1981, 145), and Grassini (1981, 71), believe that the difficulty in devising a theory of SOEs lies in their multiple, conflicting, and confusing objectives. Raiffa suggests the possibility of a trade-off between different objectives. The problem, according to him, is not only the multiple and conflicting objectives but also the dispersion of power in the SOEs. To reiterate, the behavior of the SOEs is constrained and dependent upon the behavioral structure of political forces. As a result, these embodied, problematic structures of the SOEs become intensified by changes in the government. This, in turn, may change the objectives, or, as Noreng (1981, Chapter 9) pointed out, multiple them. According to Aharoni's (1981, Chapter 13) view, the inability to identify an objective function for the SOE is not the result of democratic participation, but of a combination of other interrelated factors.

Furthermore, the lack of financial targets and the availability of capital at low or no cost handicap us because these affect our technological choices and the scale of operations and disregard elements of risk. Vickers and Yarrow (1988, 147) believe that overinvestment and internal inefficiencies of SOEs resulted, in large part, from deficiencies in the overall framework of control. However, the former and latter consequences could be related to social functions of SOEs. Consequently, their price formation and investment criteria do not follow the rules of a market system. This, too, creates some problems for posing applicable theoretical propositions. Another factor that affects the economic theory and behavior of SOEs is related to managerial discretion. The imposition of different restrictions and objectives on the management of private and public enterprises prevents them from having the same managerial discretion. Therefore, managerial behavior in the private enterprises and SOEs would be different, and the same behavioral function and economic theory could not be applied to both. In view of all these complicating factors, we have a problem not only in developing a theoretical framework but also in its application to SOEs.

Expansion of Mixed Enterprises

In the preceding section, we have suggested that it would be more appropriate to consider SOEs in an oligopolistic, not monopolistic, framework. Here, we now consider another aspect of these enterprises.

During the last few decades, especially in some European countries, many SOEs exist in partnership with private enterprise. Such joint ventures, commonly called mixed enterprises, have shown a considerable rate of growth in the past. The motives and reasons for this expansion are numerous, and there is no clear pattern to explain their existence. We shall discuss only a few of the more important ones.

Firstly, sharing investment between private and public enterprises would spread the risk and reward between government and private sectors, and both would achieve greater security. By looking at mixed enterprises from this perspective, the role of SOEs becomes even more important, especially when the investment requirement is large. The sharing of ownership between private and public enterprises makes financing easier. Such partnerships are usually encouraged when the SOEs want to enter into diversified industries or expand investment in already existing enterprises. Considerable support for this reasoning is found in most European countries--witness the partnership of private enterprises and SOEs in French motorways, the North Sea oil industry in the U.K., and the offshore gas industry in the Netherlands.

Secondly, the growth of mixed enterprises in most countries, especially in the western European community, is related to historical and political factors. In some countries, the government's take-over of industries has been subjected to protracted public debate. In Italy after World War II, for example, the control of industries by the government was viewed as "remnant fascism" and "fascist legacy" by the Liberal Party, some factions of the Christian Democratic Party, private business managers, and some economists (Martinelli 1981, 88-89). Several organizations believed that social goals would not be attained if the control remained in the hands of private enterprise since one of its major goals has been to maximize profits. The lack of agreement among various groups forced them to compromise their positions regarding the role of the state in the economy. This, in turn, gave impetus to the growth of mixed enterprises.

Thirdly, another factor that has contributed to the growth of mixed enterprises is the technological needs of both private and public enterprises. To encourage innovative growth within companies, private financial and credit institutions more readily provide necessary funds to mixed enterprises, such as the National Research and Development Corporation and the National Enterprise Board (U.K.), the *Institute de Development Industriale* (France), and the National Investment Bank (Netherlands). The expenditures of some of these enterprises (e.g., defense and aerospace) on research and development also depend upon government funds.

Lastly, the growth of mixed enterprises has also occurred as a consequence of the inability of some of the private enterprises to repay public loans from the government. In such cases, the government simply became a shareholder to the extent of money owed by private enterprises. The share of government in the steel industry in Belgium and shipbuilding in other European countries are examples of this occurrence.

Extent of SOEs

If we wish to compare the importance of SOEs in the economies of various countries, using the number of such enterprises can be highly misleading, because these numbers depend on how each country defines an SOE. Some, such as Austria and Spain, consider all enterprises as state-owned when public ownership is fifty percent or more. Other countries, like Britain and France, use additional criteria besides ownership (such as degree of government control) to classify enterprises as state-owned. Furthermore, the inclusion or exclusion of SOE subsidiaries also makes a significant difference in the number of SOEs reported by each country. Furthermore, a small number of enterprises could have a large share of employment, sales value, etc., in the economy. For example, among the 500 largest companies in the world in 1980, if we use volume of sales as an index, fifty-four were public enterprises. If the same index were applied to 100 of the largest of these 500 outside the United States, eighteen would be public enterprises (Fortune 1981, 206-218). Table 1.1 shows the number of public nonfinancial enterprises in OECD countries in 1980.

SOEs' areas of activities differ from country to country. In most European and developing countries, some of the sectors, such as postal services, telecommunications, and public utilities, are outright government monopolies; in others, governments hold the largest shares but do not have monopoly control. SOEs are important in traditional industries in part because of economies of scale and density economics. There are some industries in which the roles of SOEs in investment or output is negligible because of small-scale operations, such as agriculture, hunting, fishing, and forestry. However, the share of SOEs in such sectors is greater in developing countries than in industrial ones. For example, in Tunisia, Turkey, and

TABLE 1.1
Number of Public Nonfinancial Enterprises in OECD Countries

No. of Enterprises	Countries
1-10	France, Italy, Luxembourg
11-20	United States, Belgium, Netherlands
21-30	Canada, Australia, New Zealand, Finland, Ireland
31-40	Japan, Denmark, Greece, Turkey, United Kingdom
41-50	Germany, Iceland, Norway
51-100	Austria, Sweden
101 or more	Portugal, Spain

Source: *Government Finance Statistics Year Book*, 1980, International Monetary Fund, Washington, D.C., 1980.

Taiwan, the share of SOEs is 18.3, 15.4, and 13.4 percent respectively, but in Austria, Australia, and France, it is 3 percent, .01 percent, and 0 percent respectively (Short 1983, 18-19). Also, in the case of manufacturing industries, the share of SOEs in terms of output or investment is greater in developing countries than in industrialized ones. Political, economic, and historical reasons account for the prevalence of these large shares. In most developing countries, industries such as coal and petroleum are owned and operated by the government. Similarly, sectors such as leather, footwear, wood products, and hotel industries have considerable government ownership and control in developing countries, but they are not a part of the government sector in industrialized countries.

Conclusion

To summarize, it is clear that SOEs are primarily engaged in a handful of capital-intensive industries. In the following chapter, we demonstrate that the percentage share of public enterprises in total capital is greater than the percentage share they contribute to GDP. In the process of this, analysis, we shall address the following questions: Is capital intensity directly related to the nature of industries run by SOEs? Is the capital requested necessary, or is the demand for capital artificially inflated because of the lower cost of capital? Do the SOEs have the necessary freedom to make decisions regarding the size of their labor force and wages, or are these influenced by political pressures?

2

Investment Criteria for SOEs

How investment decisions are made or should be made in SOEs is an important question. In this chapter, we shall investigate whether it is appropriate to utilize the same investment criteria for the SOEs as are applied to private enterprise. The factors and restrictions that prevent us from applying the same criteria to both and the consequences of such applications are also analyzed.

If we look at the issue of efficient allocation of resources and adopt the position of welfare economists (i.e., the Pareto optimality condition) the marginal rate of return (MRR) on investment projects should not only be equal between private and public enterprises but also within them. If the opportunity costs were different between and within public and private enterprises, social welfare could be improved by a reallocation of investment (Heald 1980, 245). This argument would be correct if and only if both private and public enterprises operate under the same conditions and restrictions and if they have the same goals. The Pareto optimality conditions may not always be satisfied. For instance, if private investment fails to reflect social time preference rate (STPR), it could be argued that the equality of the rate of return between private and public enterprises is not a necessary condition for efficient allocation of resources. Therefore, investment decisions in the public sector may not be based on the same rate of return and the same discount rate criteria as are applied to private enterprises. Here, we are not arguing against the application of realistic financial tests for SOEs, but we do hold that these tests should take into account the restrictions imposed on the autonomy of SOEs by institutional, political, and economic constraints. The existence of different constraints may well make the tools of private financial tests inapplicable to the SOEs, unless the inclusion of all possible constraints is feasible.

Price formation and investment decisions are interrelated. Inaccuracy in one affects the accuracy of the other. For example, the use of an SOE to achieve public policy, specifically designed to stimulate demand by keeping prices below the costs of production, is bound to give rise to a need for more investment. A lack of realistic investment criteria could result in an unnecessary expansion of investment and output. Engaging the SOEs in capital-intensive industries gives an opportunity to charge a price above the costs of production. There may also be an opportunity to practice price discrimination. Using SOEs as a tool of public policy may prevent them from charging whatever the market will bear. Whenever political and economic objectives are interwoven, economic efficiency becomes a secondary goal. There are cases where the primary objective is not the efficient allocation of resources, but really an attempt to gain control of capital resources (Granick 1976, Chapter 5). Many different investment criteria have been used for decisionmaking by SOEs. A summary of the main criteria, with their advantages and disadvantages, is presented in Table 2.1. This chapter concentrates on the two major criteria: the Test Discount Rate (TDR), or Net Present Value (NPV), and the Required Rate of Return (RRR). The second criteria is known under a variety of names, including Discounted Cash Flow (DCF), Marginal Efficiency of Capital (MEC), and Internal Rate of Return (IRR). The analysis of these two criteria is based on the experience and data of the U.K.

Test Discount Rate (TDR)

The need for a TDR arises whenever it is necessary to evaluate decisions involving streams of costs and benefits accruing at different points in time. Discounting enables costs and benefits to be expressed in terms of equivalent value today. The NPV is derived by discounting the cash receipts to their present values, summing them over the life of the proposal, and deducting the initial outlay (See Table 2.1). A project would pass the TDR test if its NPV is zero or larger when the real flows are discounted at the TDR, or if the IRR on the project is equal to or greater than the TDR. The discount rate that was used for the SOEs in the U.K. during the early 1960s was referred to as the TDR. The primary objective for using the TDR was to promote consistent investment appraisal, and it was believed that the application of the TDR would promote a more efficient allocation of funds. The opportunity cost of investment in the private sector was used as the pacesetter for investment decisions in public enterprises. The 1967 White Paper stated that in the evaluation of investment projects by nationalized industries the use of the DCF technique and the TDR was required (Treasury 1967, Cmnd 3437). The TDR had to be sufficient to ensure that resources were used efficiently and had to be no less than the minimum expected rate of return on a marginal low risk project undertaken for commercial purposes.

The use of opportunity cost of investment in private enterprise is not an adequate guideline for decisions about investment in SOEs. State and

TABLE 2.1
Investment Criteria

CRITERIA	FORMULA	ADVANTAGES	BASIC WEAKNESSES
Payback	$P = \frac{I}{NCF}$ P: Payback Period I: Initial Investment NCF: Average Net Cash Flow	- The simplicity of calculation - Excellent indicator of cash recoverability	- The limited period of time taken into account - Ignores the time pattern of receipts
Net Present Value	$NPV = K_0 + \sum_{t=1}^{n} \frac{(B_t - C_t)(1 + dI)^t}{(1 + r + R)^t (1 + dE)^t}$ R: Risk premium to allow for uncertainty dI & dE: Annual anticipated rates of inflation by investors and decision makers respectively B: Benefit at time t C: Cost at time t K_0: Initial capital r: Discount rate n: Relevant time horizon	- Permits the use of different r's - Time periods allow for budget constraint and capital rationing - Allows for variation in scale of projects - Enables planners to choose between projects - Arrives at a unique solution	- Major shortcoming is a need to select r (the social discount rate) - This criterion does not necessarily guarantee the attainment of maximum social welfare if income distribution is one of the primary objectives of SOE (Webb 1973) - Uncertainties (i.e., technical and market) and lack of complete information make the calculation of NPV as an unreliable investment criterion (Semmler 1985, 20)
Internal Rate of Return (also known as Required Rate of Return and Marginal Efficiency of Capital)	Solve for P $IRR = \sum_{t=0}^{n} \frac{(B_t - C_t)}{(1 + P)^t} = 0$	-Eliminates the need for a social discount rate -Can rank projects on the basis of IRR and can select projects until the budget is exhausted -Requires less information than the NPV approach	-May have multiple solutions -Not a consistent criterion if projects are mutually exclusive -When comparing IRR and NPV, we may find inconsistency at very high interst rates -IRR provides no guidance for the optimal scale of project when such a scale can be defined -Cannot use IRR to reflect the scarcity of funds over time

TABLE 2.1 (continued)

CRITERIA	FORMULA	ADVANTAGES	BASIC WEAKNESSES
Cost-Benefit Analysis	$MBC = \sum_{t=0}^{n} \frac{\frac{B_t}{(1+r)^t}}{\frac{C_t}{(1+r)^t}}$	-B/C ratio is satisfactory for independent projects	-The determination of a suitable social discount rate which costs and benefits are relevant and how they should be valued -The need to measure surplus value with adequate knowledge of individual preferences -The accuracy of this analysis is inversely related to the scale of the activity
Annuity Method (Annual Capital Charges)	$T = \frac{K(1+r)^n}{(1+r)^{n-1}}$ T: Total annual capital charges K: Capital cost of the project n: Relevant time horizon		-Assumes that the capital cost components, interest rates, and depreciation are held constant -Externalities may complicate the problem of evaluating benefits -Fails to evaluate the effects of operating costs
Profit Margin (Neo-Schumpeterian) (See Semmler 1985)	$r_j = \frac{[P(I - A^o)]_j}{[PB]_j} = \frac{n_j/c_j}{[PB]_{j/c_j}}$ P: Price vector I: Identity matrix A: Matrix of input coefficient B: Matrix of fixed capital n_j/c_j: Profit margin $[PB]_{j/c_j}$: Ratio of fixed capital to cost of production n: Vector of average profit per unit of output	-Take into account uncertainties -Higher short run profit margin is more realistic (Semmler 1985, 20)	

private enterprises do not operate under the same structural constraints and objectives, and they do not operate on the same trading basis. The concept of opportunity cost itself is not without conceptual and measurability problems, especially if there is a divergence between private and social costs or benefits. Bradford (1975, 887-889) and Fleming (1977, 50) argue that, if the government has the opportunity to invest in the private sector and costs and benefits of these investment projects by nationalized industries are cashable, the appropriate discount rate would be based on the social opportunity cost of capital. Webb (1979, 124) argues that the TDR as a discount rate should be theoretically acceptable if the externalities of investment projects are cashable or at least if the cashables dominate the noncashable. Webb's argument may be rejected on the grounds that, in practice, to place monetary value on all externalities is impossible.

SOEs are usually engaged in industries in which their investments have "lumpy" characteristics. This may be the result of either technological characteristics or wide fluctuations in the demand for their output. In some SOEs, inefficiency may be unavoidable, especially in those where there is a peak and an off-peak in the level of demand (e.g., electricity and postal service). Since the TDR is based on ex-ante returns in private enterprises, it is not clear how the TDR should be used in SOEs when there is capital rationing, uncertainty, NCOs, and inflation because these factors will tend to distort investment decisions. The ex-ante rate of return in a private enterprise is based on the entire investment, not a portion of it. Also, there is usually a divergence between the ex-ante and ex-post rates of return. Why should the opportunity cost of capital in the private sector be used as a yardstick for investment decisions for an SOE when it typically does not even take the whole investment into account? Why should the SOE take the ex-ante rate of return as a point of reference and not the ex-post rate? The use of the discount rate of private enterprises for the SOEs may underestimate society's preference between the present and future. On average, SOEs have been more capital-intensive than other sectors of the economy; they have a high ratio of fixed over variable capital. These and other dissimilarities in structural characteristics, circumstances, and needs between private enterprises and SOEs make the use of the discount rate by private enterprise unsuitable for the evaluation of SOEs.

The TDR has never been completely relied upon for the entire investment of SOEs in the U.K. The reason for this partial implementation of the TDR stems from the belief that some part of the investment in SOEs is necessary and essential. The "essentiality of the investment" argument rules out a more efficient use of funds in favor of a less efficient one because of the political need to maintain the existing quality of service. The National Economic Development Office (NEDO) report for gas, railways, postal services, and telecommunications supports the argument that the TDR has never been fully implemented, especially for investment with indirect benefits (NEDO 1976, Appendix D). Rees (1976, 18-19), for example, argues that, since the TDR is applied only to a part of the total investment and the part that is considered necessary and essential is left out, even a significant change in TDR would actually have a very insignificant effect on the volume of investment or capital intensity of an industry. For this reason, the use of the TDR as a tool for efficient allocation of resources cannot be justified. Furthermore, there is an obvious conflict between the objectives behind the use of the TDR and the "essentiality of the investment" argument. A better approach might be to use input-output analysis.

Required Rate of Return (RRR)

The RRR is that rate of discount that equates the present value of the stream of net receipts with the initial investment outlay (See Table 2.1). The RRR is based on the average ex-post rate of return. The central point of reference in the case of RRR is not the opportunity cost of some investment project but the return on the entire investment program. For most nationalized industries in the U.K., RRR used as the DCF rate of return and RRR as a common discount rate has been applied in only two specific cases, namely, (a) where an SOE is engaged in producing a given output with the best available technique, and (b) when the phasing out of capital expenditure is an issue (Treasury 1978a, Paragraph 64). In all other cases, each industry was given autonomy in the use of RRR after consultations with its parent department. This freedom of choice is one of the main distinctions between the TDR (1967 White Paper) and the RRR (1978 White Paper). Heald (1980, 249) argued that giving the choice of "operating methods of investment appraisal to individual industries and their sponsoring departments was the end of a uniform discount rate." This failure to use a common discount rate resulted in a misallocation of funds and violated the conditions of welfare maximization.

Further, the RRR method is beset with problems of its own. Using different TDRs for obtaining a specified RRR also may result in the sponsor department behaving as a risk averter. In those SOEs where part of their investment is the result of NCOs, the use of RRR may not be realistic. This issue becomes even more problematic if cross-subsidization of the noncommercial part of the investment is expected from the commercial side.

Therefore, in this case, the evaluation of decisions about investment based on the RRR is uncertain, due to the weights that one assigns to social costs and benefits of NCOs. In order to reduce or eliminate some of this uncertainty, we should give serious consideration to the following questions: Should prices cover the cost of financing noncommercial investments? Which opportunity cost should be used as a basis for price formation, e.g., the opportunity cost of investment in the best private enterprises or the best public enterprises?

Decisions about investments and prices must be based on the actual costs. Whenever the objective is the comparison between private enterprises and SOEs, the calculation of true costs becomes even more important. For instance, the SOEs usually borrow at less than the going market interest rate, resulting in an underestimation of the true cost of production. The deviation of ex-post from ex-ante rates of return in the private sector, besides the conceptual problems of opportunity costs, makes the use of ex-ante opportunity cost an unrealistic base of reference for decisions about investment. For some economists, such as Heald (1980, 249) and Nelson (1976, 56-57), the real cost of investment is the opportunity cost, not the shadow prices when funds are financed externally. The interest rate that is charged by public agencies does not usually reflect this opportunity cost; it is only a shadow price. The National Loans Fund rate for nationalized industries in the U.K., for instance, is a shadow rate, not the actual rate.

Most documents published by the government are ambiguous about the investment criteria to be used for those SOEs that are engaged in both commercial and noncommercial activities simultaneously, e.g., White Papers for the U.K. From our point of view, it is necessary to separate the part of losses of an SOE that are attributable to meeting social objectives from the part that is related to inefficiency. The monetary value of some of the social objectives, such as antiinflation and overemployment, might be estimated by calculating their direct negative effect on the financial accounts of SOEs. An accurate estimation of all costs of NCOs may not be possible, especially if their impact is either indirect or unquantifiable. In such cases, assigning a proxy estimate or studying the effect of SOE activities in the framework of "linkage" model would be advisable. After the cost of these NCOs has been taken into consideration, SOEs should be as efficient as their private counterparts. Otherwise, any difference could be attributed to inefficient operation. Unless a distinction is made between costs of NCOs and inefficiency, the belief that SOEs do maximize social well-being is unrealistic. The reason for such a harsh position is the possibility of providing NCOs by alternative means with lower investment needs. Our position on this issue, as discussed above, is different from those of other economists, such as Rees (1976, 18), Smith (1979, 10), Webb (1979, 124), and Heald (1980, 243).

Heald's argument for welfare maximization is based on a unique TDR for each SOE. Webb criticized the RRR and argued that the RRR compared to the TDR is inferior and less satisfactory because the RRR does not fully consider the social opportunity cost and STPR. Rees's criticism of RRR is based on its inconsistency with the opportunity cost rationale. Smith takes a position similar to that of Heald. He argues that if a unique discount rate is not universally applied, there could be a possibility of accepting an investment proposal from one SOE while rejecting a proposal from another. This would be a clear example of the misallocation of investment within the public sector itself. We, however, believe that under certain circumstances a discriminatory TDR or RRR might be necessary because of the different structural characteristics of the SOEs. In those cases in which the direct estimation of the cost of social objectives and inefficiency is not possible, the indirect method may be utilized. For this purpose, in the absence of any direct method, we recommend the following proxy estimation procedure since even a proxy measure is better than no measure at all.

A proxy estimation of cost can be obtained if a comparison is made with a similar domestic or foreign producer subject to the constraints of social objectives. A proxy measure becomes even more important when there is capital rationing. By reckoning the cost of inefficiency and social objectives, not only can we improve the well-being of the present generation but also that of future generations. The Nora report indicates that in France "sixty percent of actual subsidies had social purposes and forty percent were largely blind transfer," for which intentions were not clear and receivers were poorly indicated (Nora reports, quoted in Sheahan 1976a, 156). MacAvoy, Stanbury, Yarrow, and Zeckhauser (1989, 72) argue that explicit subsidies in Europe are enormous (around 3 percent of GDP in Italy and 1 percent in Germany and France in the early 1980s; the Italian subsidy would be around $150 billion per year on a U.S. scale).

SOEs are overwhelmingly engaged in highly capital-intensive industries, and their capital-intensity ratios, on average, have been greater than those of other sectors of the economy; however, they have accounted for a smaller fraction of the GDP, i.e., national total output. The amount of capital required by various SOEs depends on the nature of the sector or industry in which they are engaged, and they may dominate wherever economies of scale exist. In 1970, the Korean SOEs were three times as capital-intensive as the country's economy as a whole (6.56 versus 2.09), more than double that of Korean manufacturing (3.02), and approximately triple that of the nonagricultural economy (2.35). Of eleven sectors with a capital intensity above 5.0, SOEs produced almost all the output in four, and in six they had significant market share between 10 to 50 percent (Jones 1975, 123-125). Capital intensity (k) is estimated by the ratio of (IP/IT) to (OP/OT), where IP/IT and OP/OT represent percentage share of SOEs in total capital formation and in GDP at factor cost, respectively. The symbols IP and IT denote the SOEs capital formation and total capital formation in the society. Contribution of SOEs in GDP and total GDP at factor costs are shown by OP and OT, respectively. The results are presented in Appendix A2.1. A summary of the first column of this Appendix is presented in column 1 of Table 2.2. It shows that SOEs in all countries are capital-intensive (K>1), and this ratio in developing countries is almost triple that of industrial nations (3.13 versus 1.15).

We believe that an accurate calculation of the cost of capital is very important, regardless of whether or not an SOE is obligated to achieve some NCOs in addition to commercial goals. The unconditional provision of capital without taking into account all its costs may result in overcapitalization and overexpansion of an SOE. This is a harmful policy because it may interfere with both the efficient allocation of resources and the public policy goals that the SOE is expected to carry out, e.g., growth, anti-inflation, etc. Sometimes capital is provided at low cost in order to justify more political interference by the government in the operations of the SOEs. The consequences of providing capital at low cost, such as overexpansion and the resulting distortion of intersectoral allocations of funds, have been pointed out by Lewis (1952), Burn (1958), Ramanadham (1959), Dennison (1958), Munby (1959), Cairncross (1958), and other economists. Several of these economists are in favor of the equality of interest rates between the private sector and SOEs (Dennison and Cairncross), and others are not. Some of the reasons why the equality of interest rates between private enterprises and SOEs are neither necessary nor advisable are explained below.

The same risk premium cannot be used for both private enterprises and SOEs because of partial or total guarantees for the financial obligations of SOEs by the government. The difference in the structural characteristics of SOEs may justify inequality of the interest rate between private enterprises and SOEs. For instance, the government may use an SOE as a

TABLE 2.2
Percentage Share in Gross Fixed Capital Formation to Percentage Share in GDP at Factor Cost and Vice Versa

	$\frac{IP/IT}{OP/OT}$	$\frac{OP/OT}{IP/IT}$
"World" (average)	1.42	.70
Industrial Countries	1.15	.86
Developing Countries	3.13	.31
Africa	1.85	.54
Asia	3.46	.26
Western Hemisphere	3.40	.29

Source: This table is derived from "The Role of Public Enterprises: An International Statistical Comparison" published in *Public Enterprises in Mixed Economies: Some Macroeconomic Aspects*, R. H. Floyd, C. S. Gray, and R. P. Short, International Monetary Fund, Washington, D.C., 1984, Table 1, p. 120.

political tool, and political intervention risks the financial and economic viability of the SOE.

The equality of interest rates between the private enterprises and SOEs is an inaccurate guideline for comparison of allocative efficiency of capital, unless a justification can be found for the difference in the structural characteristics of the two kinds of enterprises. The use of opportunity cost of capital in the private sector as a guideline for investment decisions in the SOEs is inaccurate due to ambiguities in the opportunity cost concept. Furthermore, the cost of capital depends on its source, and the accounting procedure concerning depreciation may also influence the acceptance or rejection of an investment.

These arguments reject the equi-marginality condition between private enterprises and SOEs, but do not necessarily mean the acceptance of an inefficient utilization of resources. If we assume that the low interest rates for SOEs are reflected in their social obligations, the calculation of costs should be based on a weighted average of their liabilities from different sources. This approach might be preferable to other approaches because it would avoid some of the measurement problems. Data are readily available, and no adjustment is needed because this method also eliminates the need to compare public and private sectors. Even if part of the planned investment were financed from internal surpluses, the weighted average could still be applied.

This weighted average approach suffers from some defects. First, if there is a deviation in interest rates among financing sources, the weighted average will be sensitive to the percentage share of finances derived from each. Second, the weighted average may conflict with an efficient allocation of resources. With the weighted average approach, marginality or Pareto optimality conditions may not be satisfied, an unsatisfactory state from the neoclassical point of view. This may be the result of a divergence between opportunity costs and weighted average interest rates. If and only if we assume that lower interest rates for SOEs are justified by their social obligations, the use of the weighted average is acceptable even when the necessary conditions for the efficient allocation of resources are not satisfied.

Some Alternative Approaches to Determining the Rate of Discount in SOEs

There are two fundamental problems in making decisions about investment in public enterprises: (1) how to evaluate costs and benefits and (2) how to determine an applicable and appropriate discount rate. Several solutions to the second problem have been proposed by economists, but none is free from shortcomings. These solutions are discussed below.

The use of opportunity cost as an equivalent rate for discounting has been developed by Hirschleifer (1964). He argues that investment in public enterprises displace an equal amount of private investment, so the MRR in the private enterprises should be used for evaluating public investment. Day (1963) argues that positive or negative adjustments should be made to this opportunity cost whenever it is used as a means of discounting. Several objections may be adduced against the applicability of opportunity cost as a method of discounting. The MRR for comparable private investments might not be available, and even if it were, it may have been overestimated. In other words, if the rate is based on an unsatisfactory conventional formula, the estimated rate may be too high, and to use it as a base for discounting would be misleading (Neild 1964).

SOEs are, by and large, involved in long-lived projects. In estimating the opportunity cost of their investments, any comparison must be made only with similar long-lived private enterprises, assuming that such comparisons are free from theoretical and measurement problems, when, in fact, they are not (Dryden 1964). The results of such an estimation may still lead to multiple and often diverging rates (Henderson 1968, 105). It might not even be possible to find a comparable private industry whose opportunity costs could be used as a pacesetter for decisions in the SOEs.

Hirschleifer's assumption that public investment projects must be treated as displacing an equivalent amount of private investment is not necessarily a realistic one because a public investment could just as well be displacing either private and/or government consumption. Furthermore, public investment may appear to be inferior to private investment when the comparison is based only on monetary yields; it may well be superior when social benefits are also considered. If the opportunity cost of private investment is used as an appropriate guideline for decisions about investment in SOEs, then naturally many socially desirable investments will be rejected. From this viewpoint, a single criterion for decisions about investment must be rejected in favor of a dual standard.

Another approach for ascertaining the appropriate discount rate considers the STPR. In this approach, the substitution of present consumption for future consumption is evaluated by the government. But this approach, much like the first, may be criticized for its restrictive assumptions and consequent inapplicability because it is based on subjective values assigned by the government to future consumption vis-à-vis present consumption. STPR is a very information-intensive approach. The correct and timely information is crucial for arriving at an accurate STPR. For instance, the form of the utility function, the socioeconomic structure of society (age, growth of population, growth of income), and capital rationing must all be considered. Any actual or assumed changes in these variables would change the estimated value of the STPR and create multiple STPRs or even a range of possible rates. Another problem with the STPR arises when capital rationing is prevalent. In this case, a project might pass the financial test (e.g., NPV>0) but because of capital rationing it cannot be undertaken. Thus, cancellation of investments in some SOEs might become necessary unless a higher STPR were adopted. These shortcomings led some economists, such as Henderson (1968, 102), to conclude that "it is a waste of time to try to arrive at a rate of interest for use in the public investment decisions by STPR."

A third approach for deriving a suitable interest rate for the evaluation of investments by SOEs is based on a combination of the first two approaches. This has been suggested by Feldstein (1964) and Marglin (1963). In this approach, the net benefits of an SOE must be discounted by a predetermined STPR and then compared with the social opportunity cost of capital. Only if the NPV of an SOE, when discounted by this STPR, is greater than the social opportunity cost of capital should the investment be undertaken. However, this approach is extremely complex and still has all the shortcomings of the other two approaches (Henderson 1968, 107-118).

The final approach uses the interest rate on long-term government bonds as an appropriate discount rate for evaluating investment in SOEs. Day (1963, 40) advocates this approach. His recommendation has been criticized by Marglin (1963) and Feldstein (1964). Henderson (1968, 97) concludes that "the choice of the government bond rate may be regarded as a last resort, the outcome of despair of the possibility of reaching a result by another route." Some of the factors that might diminish the significance of this interest rate on long-term bonds as a discounting factor could include the expected rate of inflation and the risk of bond market price changes, domestic monetary policy, and international monetary flows. Furthermore, the interest rate on long-term bonds may not fully reflect how much the present generation is willing to sacrifice for the future.

In summary, none of the above approaches is satisfactory and conclusive, and each of the four alternatives has encountered a great deal of criticism. These difficulties should not, however, prevent the decision-makers from specifying some rate of interest for discounting. Unspecified rates might result in inferior methods of investment appraisal. The interest rate for discounting should be explicit because the level of interest rates can and does affect not only the total amount of investment but also its composition. These approaches, as already pointed out, are subjective, and they may not be readily applicable to SOEs.

Most of the investment criteria discussed above rely on the concepts and rationale used for private enterprise. But can the standards set for private enterprise be applied to SOEs? SOEs do not have the same structural characteristics and are not subject to the discipline of market forces found in the private sector. We believe SOEs should not act as commercial entities and seek to earn a commercial rate of return comparable to their private counterparts, unless they are completely free of any social obligations. Their social obligations and politically based decisions make a single criterion inappropriate. Investment criteria for SOEs should be based on social values, not merely economic ones. Criterion "packages" are more appropriate than any single criterion, such as the TDR or IRR. A different package should be tailored for each SOE, subject to the constraints and restrictions that may be imposed on its activities. The SOEs', investment should not be measured in terms of financial viability because this ignores social and indirect benefits. SOEs could, quite often, achieve financial viability simply by raising their prices, especially when they are engaged in capital-intensive industries where they might have considerable monopoly power.

Treatment of Risk and Uncertainty

Both state-owned and private enterprises are engaged in risky and uncertain activities. How should these uncertainties be treated? One common procedure is the integration or adjustment of risk premiums into the discount rate, which is not a difficult task. The major problem is determining the size of this risk premium. Theoretically, uncertainty could be based on a compounding function of time, but whether such a compounding assumption would be true requires additional empirical research. Most of the SOEs have a long life expectation, and this affects their cash flow expectations. If a higher discount rate is a reflection of risk premiums, then the results might be biased against capital-intensive industries.

Next, we take up the questions of what kind of risk should be included and whether such a risk premium should be adopted for both private and public enterprises. An exact and scientific measure of the risk premium depends upon the availability of suitable data. In assessing the true risk premium, knowledge concerning "economic risk" is important. The economic risk refers to the probability of marginal investment in alternative uses and the social return in those alternatives. The problem is to determine which alternative we are referring to, such as private, public, or similar foreign industries. If economic risk is taken into account, investment in most SOEs would be rejected. Thus, the inclusion of a premium for economic risk in an SOE usually is not considered because the economic viability is not the only criterion for most investment in these SOEs. Social and other needs are often the key factor in making investment decisions. The opposite is true in the case of private enterprises because they are mainly concerned with their economic and financial viability.

If we assume that borrowing by SOEs is guaranteed by the government and that lenders are really risk averters, lenders should finance the SOEs at lower interest rates than those charged to private enterprises. This argument is based on differences in the "social variability" (Hirschleifer 1966, 252-276). The impact of social variability (e.g., of war, depression, etc.) on the SOEs is less than that on the private enterprises. Thus, from Hirschleifer's point of view, lower risk premiums and lower capital costs for SOEs are justifiable because of their lower social variability. This argument would not hold if lenders assumed that the government may change its attitude regarding the financing of its obligated payments. Private lenders may include the impact of government policies (e.g., fiscal and monetary) in their interest rate. Thus, the nominal interest rate that lenders charge SOEs may, in a sense, include the effect of social variability. If the lenders do not behave in this manner, they have only minimized their risks, not completely eliminated them. We see the lender as a "partial risk averter," not a "total risk averter." The government, by taking into account a risk premium for social variability, could estimate the true social costs of capital. To disregard the full impact of social variability on the investment of SOEs will cause the displacement of private enterprises by SOEs.

Some economists, such as Baumol (1968, 788), Samuelson (1964, 93-96), and Vickrey (1964, 88-92), have utilized the law of large numbers (LLN) for comparing the costs and integration of risk between private enterprises and SOEs. The difference among these economists lies in their use of the LLN in private and/or public enterprises. They are in agreement on the use of LLN as it applies to the entire public sector and also to an individual SOE. If the LLN were applied to both the public and private sectors, then the divergence in risk would disappear. Based on LLN, the spread of investment over a large number of projects would reduce the variance in the stream of income. Samuelson and Vickrey concur that investment is less risky in the public sector than in the private sector, because risk can be spread to a greater extent in the former.

The position of Samuelson and Vickrey may not be fully acceptable because the use of LLN for only the public sector leads to a biased conclusion with respect to the private sector. Baumol points out, and we concur, that both sectors operate in a risky world and undertake risky activities; therefore, they should both be subject to LLN. As a result, he concludes that both types of enterprises face the same amount of risk, but he does not argue in favor of an equality of interest rates between them. The inequality in interest rates is the result of lenders' behavior regarding the significance of risk in the two kinds of enterprises, creating a discrepancy in the interest rates between them. Furthermore, spreading the funds over a large number of investments is not apt to reduce the variance in the stream of income, unless the spreading of investment is in diversified industries.

Arrow and Lind (1970, 364-378), among others, argue in favor of a lower discount rate for public investment. The cornerstone of their argument is the spreading of the risk over a large number of taxpayers. The result is a negligibly small burden or incidence on any one individual. Arrow and Lind believe that in comparing private and public investment the relevant factor is the expected rate of return minus the costs of risk-bearing, not the expected rate of return per se. Based on the Arrow-Lind argument, even if the expected rate of return from public investment is less than that from private investment there would still be a net gain to society. Thus, the equi-marginality condition is not necessary for efficient allocation and improvement of social well-being.

If the risk premium depends on the systematic risk of cash flow, then the risk premium for SOEs must be higher than that of private enterprises. This conclusion is based on such structural characteristics of the SOEs as capital intensity and longer life investment. Therefore, if the cash flow argument were used for decisions about investment in an SOE, most of the investment would not take place. If the objective for investment by the SOEs is social optimality, then, in addition to the appropriate discount rate and risk premium, factors such as price and scale of operation should not be ignored. A careful and proper consideration of all possible constraints must be undertaken before any attempt to explain the behaivor of SOEs is made.

Conclusion

After reviewing the works of different economists, such as Arrow and Lind (1970), Posner (1977), Peston (1977), Rees (1974), and Lintner (1981), as well as government guidelines in England, we have arrived at the following conclusion: To the best of our knowledge, there is no unambiguous guideline for the treatment of risk. The granting of autonomy for making decisions about risk and the discount rate is not really a solution. In such a procedure, the element of subjectivity plays an important role. Political strength and interference by the ministries could also lead to estimates of risk that are unrealistic.

The entire sector of SOEs may be an efficient pooler of risk, but an individual SOE cannot be. If the risk of each SOE were considered separately from the rest of the SOEs, the risk might then appear very large, depending on the scale of the individual SOE. On the other hand, risk could be very small when the scale of the entire sector of SOEs is considered. A review of the literature indicates that in the screening of risky investments of SOEs, the rate of return on private capital markets with comparable risk plays a crucial role.

SOEs in most countries are engaged in those sectors that are both highly capital-intensive and expensive, a consequence of the following circumstances. When private enterprises have no incentive to invest because some involve higher risks with very long payback periods, they are often unwilling to assume such risks or accept such a low rate of cash flow. In some cases, private enterprise may be unable to finance the initial fixed capital requirements. In other cases, the government may wish to control "commanding heights" industries. These strategic industries serve the needs of forward and backward linkages. The scarcity of capital suggests that investment decisions must be based on the MEC. However, if MEC is used as a criterion for decisions about investment in SOEs, then many investments currently undertaken will have to be dropped because their direct contribution to the national income may be negligible, due to the fact that some investments in SOEs are based on needs and indirect contributions rather than efficiency.

In some countries, the division of enterprises between private and state is based on capital intensity, as, for example, in Algeria, Ethiopia, India, and Brazil. There is no objection to such a division, but this gives rise to two important questions: First, is there any contradiction between the engagement of the state in capital-intensive industries and other objectives, such as maintaining full employment? (This issue is important especially for those countries that have redundant labor.) Second, would it be possible to improve the leverage of resource use by reducing the amount of capital involved? The use of SOEs to achieve public policy aims may often stimulate demand, especially when prices are kept below costs. This, in turn, creates an apparent need for still more capital investment. If the SOEs have access to low interest loans, this may lead to the choice of an excessively capital-intensive technology. The behavior function of managers of SOEs will depend upon the cost of their investment funds, especially as it affects their choice of technology and scale of operations.

The tremendous amount of capital requirements is related to the nature of the sector or industry. Appendix A2.2 shows the percentage share of SOEs either in terms of output or investment in major sectors. The share of SOEs in sectors such as agriculture, hunting, forestry, and fishing is small, but in electricity, gas, water, transportation, and communications it is high. Industry coverage is shown in Appendix A2.3. Together, Table 2.2 and Appendix A2.1 demonstrate that SOEs in all countries are capital-intensive (K>1), with the capital intensity in developing countries almost triple that of industrial nations (3.13 versus 1.15). The reason for the higher "K" in developing nations is the engagement of their SOEs in most capital-intensive industries.

3

Financing Sources for SOEs

We believe that a discussion of financing sources for SOEs is important because it is directly related to macroeconomic and financial analysis. After an exhaustive examination of existing studies, it is clear that no specific theory of finance has yet been developed for SOEs, although there are a number of theories for the public sector per se (Semmler 1983, Arrow and Lind, 1970). This lack of a precise finance theory for SOEs led us to develop a theory that is in harmony with empirical evidence.

Our theory is based on two conclusions that will be explained in Chapters 5 and 6. In Chapter 5, we will demonstrate that if SOEs were not expected to attain any NCOs their pricing would correspond to some kind of cost-plus pricing. In those cases where SOEs are obligated to attain a blend of commercial objectives and NCOs, the same pricing model should apply, but the costs accruing from NCOs should not be included in determining the prices. In Chapter 6, we describe in detail the contract plan. This plan delineates the obligations of a government to cover deficits that result from the restrictions it imposes on SOEs. A combination of both cost-plus pricing and the contract plan would provide more certainty and improve financial predictability, especially in regard to projected financing needs. SOEs operate in a dynamic world; therefore, the possibility of deviations from these projections must be considered. Based on case studies in different countries and in different time periods, we have concluded that a general rule concerning the use of a particular source of finance would not be useful as long as the government has so many different options. In this chapter, some of government's soft options that also affect macroeconomic variables will be studied. The consequences of these choices will be described at the end of this chapter, and the empirical study will be presented in Chapter 4.

Different Sources of Finance

The financial needs of SOEs arise from their social obligations as well as their engagement in risky, capital-intensive activities. These may include financing deficits, replacing equipment, expanding existing capacity, or extending the SOE into new and diversified areas of production. The availability of financing sources for SOEs is directly related to the stage of development and growth of their respective countries. In this context, public enterprise finance may be broadly defined as "mechanisms for raising funds, distributing profits, and absorbing losses" (Gillis, Jenkins, and Lessard 1982, 257).

Financing may be divided into two main categories that, in turn, may be further divided into subcategories. The sources of finance may be domestic or foreign, the latter being more important in the case of developing countries. Foreign financing may take the form of floating bond issues in overseas markets or direct borrowing from commercial banks. Yet, in other cases, international agencies or foreign governments may provide loans and other financial assistance. Domestic financing has more soft options. Bond issues may be floated in domestic markets, and loans may be sought either from commercial banks or government agencies. Equity capital may be sold domestically, but international sales of equity may create problems of control. The type of equity issued domestically may vary in order to minimize conflict between stockholders and governmental agencies because the latter may have NCOs. If the NCOs of an SOE are important, government grants may be needed to provide the necessary social capital. The government may also wish to provide operating subsidies or grant preferential tax treatment for meeting NCOs. Some of the more important of these categories are briefly described below.

Self-Financing

The internal generation of funds may be one of the most important means of financing an SOE. Appendix A3.1 shows the percentage of total funds derived from internal sources for France, Italy, U.K., and Ireland between 1965 and 1977. Financing from internal operations for Finland between 1981 and 1983 is shown in Appendix A3.2. This method of financing depends upon cost-plus pricing. When SOEs are engaged in the provision of goods and services without any close or perfect substitutes, self-financing may take advantage of monopoly pricing. If the treasury favors the reduction of lending to an SOE and/or if the SOEs want more autonomy, self-financing becomes rather important. The policymakers have to identify the portion of expenses that must be financed internally, subject to other constraints, such as prices and the desired quality of goods and services. In other words, policymakers must consider not only the issues of investment but also the identification of imposed restrictions on the activities of SOEs. The self-financing ratio could be adversely affected if SOEs overinvest in large-scale plants, which may be necessary because of the lumpiness of capital, or in smaller-scale plants, which may have been built to meet social objectives. Social objectives that encourage underpricing are also likely to generate excessive demand that, in turn, encourages overinvestment. Cyclical downturn may also result in unused capacity. In addition, the self-financing ratio may be affected by a lack of autonomy. Social objectives may require a minimum standard of services, the inefficient use of labor, and improper production techniques may ignore the problems of cost minimization.

The factors that cause financial problems are interwoven. Autonomy in pricing policies will affect the self-financing ratio. In some countries, there is a belief that keeping the price of output of SOEs below their costs of production would help in fighting inflation because, as Keynes pointed out, cost-price spirals fan the fires of inflation. Appendix A3.3 is designed to illustrate the impact of price restraints on the self-financing ratios of SOEs in the U.K. Until 1971, the financial pattern of public corporations in the U.K. was stable, and the range of internal financing varied between 25 and 45 percent of the total investment requirements for fixed assets and working capital. After 1971, a deterioration in the internal sources of financing was caused by price restraints. The comparison of internal funding to the total financial requirements of nine nationalized industries shows that by 1974 it had fallen from 53 to 17 percent (Appendix A3.4).

A comparison of the self-financing ratio in private and public enterprises of those countries for which data are available shows that in the mid-1970s this ratio was 76 percent in private and 48 percent in public enterprises. Perhaps the accuracy of these figures could be questioned because of the effect of taxes, but this much can be said with confidence: the self-financing ratio in public enterprises is lower than the ratio for private enterprises (Floyd, Gray, and Short 1984, 160). A high self-financing ratio may be related to monopolistic pricing and/or a dominant market position where a high degree of investment is necessary to maintain the firm's market share. If this is the reason, then, in order to maintain a dominant position, management efficiency must be encouraged; if this does not occur, the self-financing ratio will be adversely affected by any or all of the factors explained above. Among the economists who have argued in favor of 100 percent internal financing is Sir Roy Harrod (1958, 238-241). He argues that neither the individual taxpayer nor the government should have to provide the necessary capital for SOEs and advocates raising necessary capital by price increases because SOEs prices are already set too low. However, we may add that in cases where the internal finances of

SOEs are insufficient, the government could provide funds from different sources, such as borrowing, taxation, surplus revenue from government departments, or an expansion of the money supply. There is no general rule concerning the use of particular sources of finance. However, financing cannot be independent of monetary and fiscal policies and the overall state of the economy.

Government Transfers

Subsidies are another source of funding for SOEs. They may come either from local or central governments as a result of internationalization of markets and NCOs. The SOEs may be compensated directly by the government or indirectly by cross-subsidization. Strategic decisions about subsidies may be either ex-ante or ex-post. However, both methods will face some problems. If the subsidization is based on ex-ante criteria, it may adversely affect morale, the incentives for management, and the ability to meet financial targets. If the subsidy is based on ex-post criteria, it would create uncertainty about the sources of funding. Furthermore, the use of ex-post criteria imposes constraints on decisions about strategic planning. The dynamic nature of economies and changes in the priorities of government objectives do not permit effective projections over long periods of time. Imposing constraints upon the subsidization procedures, therefore, might decrease the time horizon for decisionmakers unless *ceteris paribus* can be safely assumed.

Social cost-benefit analysis may be an unrealistic tool for decisions about the level of subsidization. NCOs should be evaluated based on the needs of the society. The true cost of the output of an SOE cannot be judged on the basis of opportunity cost principles unless the internalization of all costs and benefits is possible. One way of estimating the amount of subsidy is to calculate the costs of NCOs if they are provided by a non-SOE. The subsidizing of SOEs to carry out NCOs may be in the form of lower expected rates of return, transfer payments, and/or the provision of social capital at less than market interest rates. However, the isolation of commercial costs from NCOs presents a problem because it is difficult to place a monetary value on all NCOs. The estimation of the cost of NCOs can only be a proxy measure that can be brought closer to the true costs if some improvements can be made in the identification and quantification of such issues as efficiency, performance, price, standards of service, systems of cost accounting, financial targets, investment criteria, and sources of financing.

Some of the factors that contribute to an imbalance in the financial performance of SOEs have been discussed in Chapter 1; NCOs are only one of them. Permanent open-ended subsidization of SOEs is not only inappropriate but also impossible as it contradicts both micro- and macroeconomic objectives for the SOEs. Subsidization might be justified if it yields sociopolitical or politico-economic gains and if the monetary value of such gains is at least equal to the amount of subsidies (United Nations 1976, 9). However, the problems involved in the quantification and monetary evaluation of some objectives, such as political ones, render this argument ineffective.

The defaults and inefficiencies of SOEs are masked in the form of higher taxes. Financing subsidies by means of taxation is not always politically or economically feasible. The continued existence of SOEs would be impossible if they were not economically and financially viable. The sale of Luxor AB (data communication and division) to a private company in Finland was the direct result of a continuous, long-term financial drain. In Sweden, financial crises in SOEs have forced the transfer of some ownership to private hands. The changes in the attitude of the Swedish government toward SOEs--more privatization and profit objectives--are similar to those that were taking place in Britain. What other options does the government have? Does the subsidization of SOEs always create a financial crisis for the government? The first question will be discussed in this chapter, and the second will be addressed in Chapter 4 on the basis of our empirical study.

The transfer of SOEs from public to private hands has been taking place in many countries. However, some of the unprofitable industries in these countries are still run by the state for the simple reason that they are either unattractive to private buyers or they have social objectives. For instance, some industries in Sweden, such as shipbuilding, have a negative value added, but they were not completely shutdown because social considerations outweighed budgetary pressures (Skandinaviska 1983, 65-67). In some cases, Swedish subsidization policies have been implemented for both SOEs and private enterprise. One of the objectives of a subsidization policy may be to protect those industries when at least part of their activities involve NCOs. The government may guarantee survival of SOEs in international and domestic markets where they must compete with foreign producers. Any type of support in such cases represents a net burden on the government revenue. The capital intensity and involvement of SOEs in the provision of social objectives have invariably contributed to their financial dependence on the government. One of the social objectives--to absorb surplus labor--might restrain the productivity growth of SOEs as compared to either their domestic or international counterparts. Vickers and Yarrow (1988, 146-147) argue that "it is not clear to what extent the observed productivity variations can be attributed to the effects of different types of ownership. Over the relevant periods, most studies of international productivity differentials have shown the U.K. lagging behind its principal competitors irrespective of whether the industry concerned was privately or publicly owned." Restraint in productivity growth would affect the degree of competitiveness of those SOEs when the demand for their output is both highly elastic and dependent upon the international market for survival. Semmler (1980, 7), based on studies of Okun and Perry (1978) and Houthakker (1979), argues that "intertemporal and cross-sectional studies show that price changes were highly negatively correlated with the growth rate of productivity."

Also, international business cycles would cause a greater increase in the trade deficit for those countries that are less competitive in international markets. There is an indirect relationship between productivity-deficits and productivity-subsidization or productivity-financial dependency. Thus, there is a conflict between micro objectives (productivity) and macro objectives (employment). If SOEs are expected to carry out NCOs and at the same time compete in international markets, their survival will inevitably depend upon government support. For instance, the survival of many Swedish and Norwegian SOEs depends upon the financial support of their respective governments. The cost of supporting Statsföretag, a Swedish state-owned limited company, was SEK 1,317.1 million between 1975 and 1982, although its sales revenues were only SEK 15.562 million (Ministry of Industry 1982, 18). It may have had an operating loss, but it was providing employment to over 46,000 people (Appendices A3.5 and A3.6). The Norwegian government owns more than 75 percent of the capital stock in SOEs, with the remainder in private hands. Direct subsidies, loans, and grant authorizations by the governments to such SOEs for 1980 to 1982 were NOK 4,055 million. Such grants increased from NOK 137 million in 1972 to NOK 2.3 billion in 1982. The expansion of these subsidies has created some financial problems for the state (Royal Norwegian Ministry of Finance, 1983, 77). For this reason, in 1983, the Industry Community Committee (also called the Burik Committee) proposed that the state-owned companies, with a few exceptions, must operate on the principle of profitability.

In order to clearly understand the reasons for subsidizing SOEs, it is important to first understand the objectives, form, length, size, and scale of subsidization. Some of the reasons for subsidies include anti-inflation objectives, employment creation, regional development, compensation for previous mistakes, and increasing the degree of competitiveness. One major form of subsidization is cross-subsidization among SOEs. For instance, in most of the EEC countries, telecommunications and postal services operate as a single entity. The profits of the former are used to compensate the losses of the latter. The second type of subsidization is in the form of transfer payments, accomplished in one of two ways--either direct transfers from the government via grants or the acceptance by the government of responsibility for financial problems of SOEs if they carry out specific NCOs. Transfers of the first type are often found in France, Belgium, and the Federal Republic of Germany, and the second type is practiced in the U.K. and other EEC countries. The latter may involve waiving some of the financial responsibilities of SOEs by prior agreement with the state (for instance, waiving the obligation of dividend payments from the Bundes Post, Salzgitter, and Viag). In Belgium, dividend payments were waived for *Societe National T. Investissement (SNI)*.

We may note here that the length, size, and scale of subsidization should be related to several factors, such as NCOs, enterprise structure, market fluctuations, and changes in priorities. Quantification of these factors should be done prior to the start of actual operations. Only after estimating the costs of NCOs should SOEs receive compensation. This estimation would be more accurate if the assumption of *ceteris paribus* could be made or if SOEs operated in vertically integrated form. Unfortunately, in most cases, neither assumption can be made. Therefore, the exact quantification of size, scale, and length of subsidization is impossible, especially over a long time horizon if the SOE in question is dependent upon either input factors or revenue sources that are external to it. The steel, chemical, and shipyard industries in England, Sweden, France, and Italy all depend upon the international market. Any crisis or fluctuation there affects their costs and revenues. However, because of NCOs, a drop in international demand may not result in a corresponding reduction in output (Skandinaviska 1983, 65). In Appendix A3.7, shifts in the production of iron ore have been shown for selected countries.

In regard to the size and duration of subsidies, we find that in some countries, such as France and Senegal, where the government is obligated to compensate SOEs for the costs of NCOs, their procedure for compensation is based on "Reversing the Burden of Proof Principle " or the "Doctrine of Improper Burdens" that will be studied in greater detail in Chapter 6. Appendix A3.8 lists the subsidies and other current transfers as a percentage of GNP for twenty countries. In Appendix A3.9, the subsidies as a percentage of revenue and of GDP are shown for the U.K. from 1967 to 1982.

Loans

Another way of meeting the financial needs of SOEs is through loans from either the government or private institutions. The loans may be used for different purposes, such as covering a deficit, financing fixed assets, or financing working capital. They may either be short-term or long-term, but the borrowers are legally obligated to pay interest charges where the actual rate of interest may depend upon capital intensity and NCOs. The interest charged to SOEs may be less than the actual cost of obtaining the capital by the government. There are cases where waiving the interest charges or temporarily suspending capital have occurred in EEC countries. For instance, in 1973 in the U.K., the debt of British Overseas Airline Corporation, British Rail, and National Coal Boards was waived (Appendix A3.10). In Appendix A3.11, capital write-offs for nine major nationalized industries are shown. In some countries (e.g., England), whenever the SOEs are unable to pay their financial obligations the government may decide to change their loans to equities. The result of such transformation is that, although they may fail to increase the actual amount of capital, they do relieve the anxieties of SOEs.

Paying interest on debt money is a legal obligation of SOEs, but this obligation may not always be enforced rigorously. In such cases, there may not be much incentive for management to improve efficiency and productivity. At the same time, SOEs are often in a better position in financial markets when compared with private enterprises because their loans are guaranteed either explicitly or implicitly by the government. Also, for the same reason, the chances of liquidation of SOEs' assets are rare when compared with private enterprises. Therefore, some indiscriminate borrowing by SOEs may take place. In many countries, especially developing nations, many of the SOEs are unable to generate enough funds to finance their capital needs. A United Nations intercountry study showed that the government is a major capital provider for SOEs (United Nations 1976, 40). In some countries, loans and share-capital are the two main financial sources, but there is no clear pattern of loan/equity ratios for the same enterprises in different countries. The dissimilarity in magnitude of each source of finance in different countries may depend on social objectives, nonrational economic decisions, capital intensity, historical, cyclical and structural fluctuations, and institutional arrangements. In some cases, such as Italy where the credit institute known as IMI is in charge of loans to SOEs, there is a definite lack of freedom to respond to a given cash flow problem. Loans to SOEs may come from either state or central government sources. For instance, in Italy, Belgium, France, and the Netherlands, funding of loans by state agencies is common. In the U.K., loans are often made by the central government. There are, however, constraints on such loans. In 1976, the "cash limit" system was introduced in the U.K. where all external sources of finance are specified at the beginning of each year. The 1978 White Paper describes the system for imposing discipline for proper financial management and as a useful step toward the objective of greater public accountability (Treasury 1978a, Paragraph 82). Changes in the cash limit were subject to ministerial agreement and parliamentary review. This system had a number of possible consequences. It encouraged more self-financing through such means as raising prices, and may also have affected the amount and proportion of fixed investment and working capital.

Equity

Equity financing may come from either public or private shareholders. Private capital plays an important role in financing SOEs in some countries, including the Federal Republic of Germany and Italy. The equity capital may be used for financing new investment or for covering deficits. Private shareholders might not be interested in buying equities that merely cover deficits unless other special circumstances exist. One way of increasing the demand for risky equities is by guaranteeing a minimum dividend on such equities. These dividends will depend upon sales volume, prices, costs, and the rate of inflation. However, if the government takes into account the rate of inflation, in some cases it may mean an implicit acceptance of its failure to achieve the expressed anti-inflation objectives.

Equity capital is preferred over loan capital by managers of SOEs, especially when the SOE is operating at a deficit, when it is obligated to pay market interest rates, or when the investment is risky. Purchases of equities may be made by either public institutions or the general public. The issues of control and income distribution resulting from ownership of equity stock are important, especially if the SOE expects a high rate of return. If the SOE owns less than 51 percent of its shares, it may be dominated by majority shareholders, and since the shareholders are interested in dividends, they may be in favor of higher prices. As a result, this shareholders' objective could conflict with the anti-inflation objectives of the government. The issue of control could be solved if the voting rights for privately owned shares were limited. Another possible disadvantage of equity capital depends upon whether the shares are sold to wealthy investors or to the workers. Thus, we note that there is definitely an interdependency between the method of financing and income distribution.

Heath (1978, 118-127) notes that one source of risky capital for some SOEs could be their undistributed surpluses. However, SOEs may be reluctant to use these in risky investments. Risk capital should be provided by the government for those SOEs that are unable to satisfy the conditions of eligibility for receiving public dividend capital (PDC). Among the industries that were eligible for PDC, British Steel has been the largest recipient of such funds--38 percent between 1974 and 1977. Others, including British Airways, British Aerospace, and British Shipbuilding, also received PDC. In Italy, equity capital in the past has been provided for both meeting operating deficits and making new investments. PDC in Italy has been offered on the basis of "need" rather than efficiency, and it is costless to the SOE. In France, provision of equity capital by the government is based on the contribution of the SOE to the social benefit, but there is nothing similar to PDC in the Federal Republic of Germany. In summary, SOEs prefer equity capital because they look upon it as a cheap source of capital or a soft option. In England, however, the treasury warned SOEs not to use equity capital as a soft option, but the warning did not have much practical effect because the capital market discipline of private enterprises could not be imposed. The dividend payments of British Airways, National Giro, and British Steel in Appendix A3.12 show that warnings by the treasury have been ineffective and that the SOEs under study look upon equity capital as entailing little or no cost. This may be one of the reasons why the treasury and successive British governments have been reluctant to extend PDC to any other SOEs that have not already used them (Treasury 1978a, Paragraph 88). Other SOEs whose capital structure is based on debt financing and retained earnings are consistently and persistently pressing to be the beneficiary users of PDC. The National Coal Board has repeatedly argued that mining is a risky activity and should be allowed to use PDC. If their capital structure were to include PDC, the result would be a lower gearing ratio-ratio of debt capital to PDC that would permit a smaller contractual obligation of interest payments on debt capital.

Raising Capital from Capital Market

Capital financing of SOEs from different sources, whether public or private, still places a burden on government finances. In England, many authorities on SOEs have argued in favor of raising long- and medium-term capital directly from the capital market without any treasury guarantees. The Herbert Committee recommended this means of capital financing for SOEs (Treasury 1956, Paragraph 353). This method has both advantages and disadvantages for the SOEs and the government. If SOEs were permitted to compete with private enterprise in the capital market, this would force SOEs to bear the opportunity cost rather than an arbitrarily specified RRR. Autonomy and freedom of action give psychological advantages to SOE managers because they feel free to borrow as if they were in private enterprise. Managerial efficiency with respect to resource allocation and financial management would be encouraged. The management would have to produce enough surplus revenue to pay interest on debt, generate sufficient earnings to serve as a source of finance, and create even more autonomy. If an SOE has to borrow in competitive capital markets on the strength of its own performance, it would inevitably eliminate many inefficiencies in operations and improve its managerial efficiency.

In the public mind, SOEs are associated with the government, and lenders find it difficult to consider them as independent financial entities. This implicit guarantee is often assumed by lenders whether or not the debt capital is issued with an explicit government guarantee. Another issue is the high elasticity of money demand by the SOEs that makes it difficult to obtain the necessary funds without government guarantees, due to either their lack of credit worthiness or their involvement in highly risky activities. SOEs may be willing to pay interest rates above the going market in order to obtain funding, but this could create future financial crises for the government. If the SOEs have to pay higher interest rates, they may increase the prices of goods and services they provide, and this could conflict with anti-inflation policies of the government. The higher interest rate also has distributional consequences that may again conflict with the government's income redistribution policies.

Foreign Borrowing by SOEs

Overseas borrowing by SOEs to finance new projects and current operations or cover deficits is common to both developing and developed nations (See Appendix A3.13). Foreign borrowing may be necessitated by capital intensity, reductions in income, or restrictions on borrowing in the domestic market. In some countries, such as Mexico and Portugal, foreign sources of financing are preferred over domestic sources because they involve less bureaucratic red tape. However, uncontrolled overseas borrowing may have adverse consequences on the economy. Effective controls are, therefore, advisable. For example, in England, starting in 1969, a small amount of fixed return capital has been raised abroad with treasury permission and government guarantees. In Portugal, SOEs, after informing the central bank, may borrow from international markets without the approval of the ministry of finance. In the Ivory Coast, regulations require consultations between SOEs and government authorities, such as the ministry of finance (Floyd, Gray, and Short 1984, 30). However, in practice, this requirement has, more often than not, been ignored. Borrowing from overseas may be cheaper than domestic borrowing when forgone income is considered, especially if the money is used for utilizing full capacity and for preventing the postponement of revenue-generating projects. In cases where the state does not have access to foreign lenders, it must either borrow from the domestic market or manipulate monetary and fiscal policies. However, the use of these policies could have adverse effects on the domestic financial market. Both fiscal and monetary policies affect the interest rate. The issue of public bonds, and their substitution in personal portfolios could be viewed as a reduction in the available, loanable funds for private capital formation. Increase in public capital accumulation by means of fiscal policy might have a crowding-out effect to some extent, and the continuation of this effect may create inflation that again conflicts with the macro objectives of SOEs. Richard and Peggy Musgrave (1989, 511) believe that this crowding-out effect could be eliminated with a suitable combination of monetary and fiscal policies.

What are the implications of foreign borrowing for the domestic economy? The impact depends upon the amount and allocation of these funds, on foreign exchange rates, and on domestic monetary policy. A series of questions may be raised regarding this issue. Is the borrowed money spent for new projects, or is it merely covering the deficits of current projects? Will it be spent on purchases of goods and services produced in the domestic market or on imports from overseas? Will it generate a new supply of foreign exchange in the long run? Is it spent on productive or unproductive activities?

It is important to know whether the borrowed money generates a future cash flow or if it is simply a burden on the rest of the economy. In studying foreign borrowing, both short-term and long-term effects should be considered. Short concluded that the debt burden is much more critical when repayments must be made in foreign exchange, thereby creating many problems for the long term (Floyd, Gray, and Short 1984, 176). His conclusions may not be fully acceptable because financing from overseas could eventually generate more foreign exchange. In the short run, financing from abroad may have a less destabilizing effect when compared with financing from domestic markets. In the long run, the effect of foreign borrowing on stabilization depends upon how the borrowed money is utilized. If it is used for unproductive objectives, it is a deadweight burden to the SOE and the economy. In this case, not only does the borrowed money fail to generate sufficient funds to repay the principal, it may also be a burden on the rest of the economy. Depending on the amount of money borrowed, the result may be a financial crisis and may conflict with social objectives.

In the last few years, borrowing by public enterprises from international capital markets has increased. This increase in the demand for foreign money depends, among other things, upon the deficits of the SOEs and their engagement in capital-intensive industries. Data from the World Bank indicate that 23 percent of the total borrowing by public enterprises between 1976 and 1978 has been from the international capital markets (World Bank 1980). Developed countries were more frequent borrowers–77 percent of gross foreign borrowing compared to 23 percent by developing nations. Partial data collected by the World Bank indicate that gross borrowing by public enterprises from international markets totaled $25 billion in 1978. Floyd, Gray, and Short (1984, 30) argue that World Bank data fail to include foreign private credit suppliers. Generally speaking, the amount of borrowing from the international market is underestimated. If the foreign borrowing of SOEs is channeled only through government accounts, this would create a problem in estimating exactly the different sources of finances. Such biased estimates of foreign borrowing are not unusual, especially in developing countries.

Debt Financing and Macro Objectives

Different ways of financing the needs of the SOEs have been discussed in this chapter. Here, we concern ourselves with the influence of SOEs' financing on the macro variables, such as inflation, interest rate, and divestiture of investment.

Debt Financing of SOEs and Inflation

In many countries, policymakers believe in keeping the prices of SOEs' outputs below their costs of production in order to curb inflation. In the U.K., Prime Ministers Edward Heath in 1970 and Harold Wilson in 1974 favored the use of such anti-inflation policies. During his election campaign, Heath declared, "I will cut out inflation at a stroke if elected" (Heath, quoted in Eltis 1979, 7). This is a monolithic, single-minded position that does not consider other causes of inflation. Those who believe that inflation is predominantly attributable to "cost-price spirals" are influenced by Keynesian economists. They completely ignore the consequences when the price of the SOEs' products are held below their costs of production. In a mixed economy, governments can impose price ceilings on SOEs, but they are unable to fully control the prices of other products and resources, especially when prices are set by market forces. Petroleum, for instance, is an essential input for many industries, but its price fluctuations are influenced by business cycles and international economic conditions. How can a government control the prices of food, clothing, etc., when there is an oil embargo?

Product prices of SOEs, if held below their cost of production, in the long run may actually accelerate the inflation rate and may also create a deficit for them. The government may have to make up this deficit either by borrowing in capital markets or by increasing the money stock. Either method of financing the deficit could result in further inflation, especially during boom periods. In regard to the inflationary impact of deficit financing by public enterprises, Floyd, Gray, and Short (1984, 31) point out that "bank credit to public enterprises is of concern primarily insofar as it exceeds normal commercial requirements. In the short run, such credit is more likely to crowd out other potential borrowers, but in the long run it seems more likely to be inflationary."

Because the lower-than-cost prices of the output of SOEs are likely to give rise to deficits in their operating budgets, it is important to take into account the methods of financing these deficits when we analyze the true effects of such price controls. The government may create credit for financing the deficits of SOEs by increasing the supply of money. The effect of such policy on overall prices could be ascertained with the help of an econometric model, if the time series data concerning the deficits of the SOEs and their relationship to money supply were available. In fact, a simple quantity theory model for this purpose was used by Gray (Floyd, Gray, and Short 1984, 87). He concludes that if it is assumed that creation of money will finance the deficit of the SOEs, a proportional increase in average prices identical to the increase in the money supply would occur. Gray used Fisher's identity equation of exchange ($MV \equiv PQ$) to arrive at this conclusion. In his formulation, M and P are the average money supply and average price index, respectively, during a year and Q is the year's GDP based on the price index. This relationship is an identity because of the ex-post assumption that V is constant, and, given this assumption, a change in M would result in corresponding changes in either P or Q or both (identity 3.2). That is,

$$\text{if} \qquad MV=PQ \tag{3.1}$$

$$\text{then} \qquad (M+\Delta M)V=(P+\Delta P)(Q+\Delta Q) \tag{3.2}$$

The effect of this change on the supply of money to finance the deficits of SOEs is shown in equation 3.3, which is derived as follows:

$$\text{or} \qquad (M+\Delta M)V=(P+\Delta P)(Q+\Delta Q)$$

$$\text{or} \qquad \frac{(M+\Delta M)V}{MV}=\frac{(P+\Delta P)(Q+\Delta Q)}{PQ}$$

$$\text{or} \qquad 1+\frac{\Delta M}{M}=1+\frac{P\Delta Q}{PQ}+\frac{\Delta PQ}{PQ}+\frac{\Delta P\Delta Q}{PQ}$$

or $$\frac{\Delta M}{M} = \frac{\Delta Q}{Q} + \frac{\Delta P}{P} + \frac{\Delta P \Delta Q}{PQ}$$

or $$\frac{\Delta M}{M} = \frac{\Delta P}{P}(1 + \Delta Q / Q) + \frac{\Delta Q}{Q} \tag{3.3}$$

Now, if changes in money supply have to give rise to a proportional change in prices, then we have to assume that the numerator of the expression $\Delta Q/Q$ is zero, i.e., ΔQ is zero. This assumption can be true only if we accept the classical postulate that the GDP is based on full employment during the year. We know this to be highly unlikely in modern economies. Gray also believes that if the deficits of SOEs are not financed by creating money, a reduction in production (a contradiction in his assumption) and some discharge of labor may become necessary. This argument is rather convoluted. The timing of deficits and increasing of money supply can be synchronized only if both are ex-ante phenomenon. If M is increased after a deficit has already occurred, then Δ M would actually influence the future deficit, not the current one. Hence, unless Gray assumes that the deficit of an SOE is predetermined, his argument concerning the ensuing change in output is not entirely realistic. As already pointed out, inflation is not monolithic but is multifaceted. Therefore, we cannot explain changes in price level by relating them to the growth of money supply alone.

In a study conducted for Argentina, Chu and Feltenstein (1978, 452-493) demonstrate that government financing of deficits by creating new money is transformed into high-powered money through the central banks. They suggest that the anti-inflation objectives of the government could be better served through control of the private sector prices. If such controls result in monetary losses for the private sector, then compensatory financing should be available through the banking system. However, since the financing of losses of the private sector by commercial banks is not rediscounted by the central banks, Chu and Feltenstein conclude that financing SOEs' deficits by increasing the money supply becomes proportionately ten times more inflationary than if the losses of the private sector had been compensated by the commercial banks. Therefore, they advocate the use of forward and backward price controls to reduce the costs of production and achieve the desired goal of curbing inflation. In summary, it may be said that the anti-inflation objective should be studied in a general, not partial, equilibrium framework. Unless the effect of NCOs on other sectors of the economy is properly assessed, the general equilibrium cannot be used.

Interest Rates

Borrowing by the government to finance the deficits of SOEs would shift the demand for loanable funds upward and result in higher interest rates. The magnitude of change in interest rate will depend on the elasticities of supply and demand for loanable funds. Also, an increase in inflation, resulting from the deficit financing of SOEs, would affect the behavior of lenders. Unless the lenders are compensated for higher inflation rates, there would be a downward shift in the supply of loanable funds. Additionally, government borrowing to finance the deficits of SOEs may have an influence on private investment. An increase in interest rates as a result of such borrowing, if all savings are used before, may raise the interest rate, and that may lead to a decline in private investment due to the so-called crowding-out effect. In sum, governmental financing of deficits could affect the interest rate structure and, thus, compound the inflationary problems.

Divestiture of Investment

Prolonged deficit financing by SOEs puts pressure on the government to seek alternatives. The "privatization strategy" is one such alternative that has been used by some countries. Privatization is not a perfect or realistic solution because it also often conflicts with other macro objectives. Complete privatization of the entire public enterprise sector is impossible for political, social, and economic reasons. Quite often, there is a lack of interest on the part of private enterprises, especially in such "crisis industries" as shipbuilding. Therefore, one needs to investigate alternative solutions. Two such alternatives are: operating the SOEs in a manner similar to that of private enterprise and diversifying SOEs into other industries.

The first alternative has been practiced in France since 1982. The second, engagement of SOEs in diversified industries and cross-subsidization among loss- and profit-making subsidiaries, is similar to the policies of some large, modern corporations. For instance, in the United States, local telephone services were subsidized by long-distance services before the breakup of AT&T. By engaging SOEs in diversified industries, the need for privatization or for changes in the level of social objectives is obviated. The costs of NCOs can be financed by the profitable activities of SOEs, raising two further concerns. It is often argued that since the SOEs are established to meet certain social objectives, they should not, therefore, indulge in profit-making activities. Further, Marxists would contend that all profit comes from surplus value generated through the exploitation of labor. This argument can be countered by noting that the issue of exploitation does not arise since the profit (i.e., the surplus value) is specifically used for enhancing the social objectives.

Conclusion

A simple and single-period criterion, such as profit, should never be considered a true indicator for measuring the performance of any SOE. In other words, "social profits," not "private profits," should be used as the proper measure of performance. In many developing and developed countries, SOEs have often been used to create "take-off conditions" or to "make a big push" in their economies. The use of SOEs to propel economic growth while trying at the same time to achieve a series of NCOs has created a series of financial problems that have often caused the SOEs to become financially dependent on alternative sources of financing. Among others, in both developed and developing countries, SOEs are engaged in stagnating and backward industries, such as shipyards and railways. These crisis-prone sectors need huge amounts of fixed and operating capital. Prolonging their operations can be justified only on grounds of social objectives, not economic ones.

In the foregoing review, we have made an attempt to find a logical explanation for varying capital structures of SOEs and to identify a theoretical framework for their financing. Some studies, such as the one done by the NEDO, have pointed to the lack of any convincing or consistent rationale for the prevalence of many different sources of finance. Furthermore, dynamic economies and changing priorities of government objectives have often frustrated economists in their attempts to develop a suitable theoretical framework to predict the financing needs of SOEs, especially over the long run. This lack of adequate finance theory for SOEs has prompted us to develop one of our own, based on contract plan and cost-plus pricing.

4

Empirical Evidence on Operating Surplus, Capital Requirements, and Debt in SOEs

In Chapter 1, we discussed the economic, political, and historical reasons for the existence and behavior of SOEs. In this chapter, we shall present the results of both our own and other empirical investigations relative to some of the main characteristics of these enterprises. Appendix A2.2 shows that SOEs are deeply involved in "heavy" industries, such as utilities, transportation, and communications, and less involved in "light" industries, such as furniture, beverages, agriculture, hunting, and forestry. Two deficiencies in Appendix A2.2 may be noted: it includes only those countries for which data were available, and the available data do not cover the same time periods for all countries.

We can draw several significant conclusions from Appendix A2.2. First, the share of "light" industries in the economies of industrially advanced countries is extremely small. For example, in the U.K., the share of "light" industries generated by SOEs in gross domestic fixed capital formation (GFCF) is zero, and in Australia, their share in the gross domestic product at factor cost (GDPF) was less than 1/4 of 1 percent. On the other hand, in developing countries, the same industries contribute a significantly large share to the GFCF. In Tunisia, Turkey, and Taiwan, these shares were 18.3, 15.4, and 13.4 percent, respectively. Second, of the total share of SOEs in either output or investment in both developed and developing nations, the bulk is accounted for by "heavy" or "capital-intensive" industries. In the U.K. and France, the shares of SOEs in terms of GFCF in electricity, gas, and water industries were 92.1 and 96.6 percent, respectively; the same shares for the same industries in Tunisia and Taiwan were 89.4 and 95.9 percent, respectively. Similarly, the share of SOEs in the same sectors in terms of GDPF in Pakistan, Korea, and India was 78.85, 81.96, and 82.73 percent, respectively. Mining and quarrying are also among the heavy industries in which SOEs are actively engaged. In Tanzania and India, the share of SOEs in these industries in terms of GDPF was 87.76 and 68.73 percent, respectively. In Senegal, in terms of gross domestic product at market prices (GDPM), and in England, in terms of GFCF, the share of SOEs in these industries was 99.20 and 26.03 percent, respectively.

Pryor (1973, 50-60) studied the nationalization ratio ("the ratio of economically active population in publicly owned enterprises and units to the total economically active population in the corresponding branch or sector") for seven major economic sectors in fifteen nations: utilities, transportation and communication, services (public administration, etc.), construction, manufacturing and mining, commerce and finance, and agriculture, forestry, and fishing. He concluded that the lowest nationalization ratios occurred in fishing, agriculture, forestry, leather products, and clothing, and the highest ratios occurred in the transportation, utilities, and communication sectors. Pryor's study also indicates that not only did the nationalization ratios in various major sectors in the economies of fifteen countries form a consistent pattern but this pattern was also seen among various branches of the same sectors. In Pryor's study, Kendall's rank order correlation coefficient (a statistic that shows the degree of correlation between two rank orderings) between fixed capital in average-sized enterprises and those nationalized enterprises engaging in manufacturing was 0.50, which is significant at the 0.05 level. A similar correlation existed between manufacturing and mining, according to a scale that ranks industries as heavy or light, and the relative degree of nationalization was 0.63, which is significant at the 0.05 level. The Kendall coefficient between fixed capital and the number of workers and employees in nationalized industries was 0.75, which is significant at the 0.05 level (Pryor 1973, 441-443). The coefficient of concordance for rank orders of capital/labor ratios in the nationalized industries of twelve nations was 0.79, which is statistically significant at the 0.05 level. From the above evidence, we may safely conclude that most SOEs are, by and large, engaged in heavily capital-intensive industries.

Another study by Smith, Hitchens, and Davies (1982, 45) supports the findings of Pryor's study. They also found that public utilities and transportation are among the most capital-intensive industries in the U.K., United States, and Germany. They further discovered that most capital-intensive industries in the U.K., such as public utilities, transportation, and communications, performed below their American counterparts because they were less capital-intensive. This might be highlighted as one of the factors responsible for differences in comparative productivity among nations.

TABLE 4.1
Comparative Productivity[a] in Public Utilities, Transport, and Communications, Averaged from 1968-1977

Year	Public Utilities		Transport	Communications
	US/UK	Germany/UK	US/UK	Germany/UK
1968-1977	3.55	1.83	2.53	1.12

Note:
a: For measuring the comparative productivity ratio, first the overall absolute productivity level (i.e., standardized net output per man) is measured as follows:

$$P = \frac{Q1 + Q2 + Q3 + \ldots + Qn}{L1 + L2 + L3 + \ldots + Ln} = \sum_{i=1}^{n} \frac{Q}{L}$$

where L, Q, 1...n denote net output, labor force, and component sectors. From dividing the relevant overall productivity levels, the comparative productivity ratio is obtained.

Source: This table is derived from Tables 12.3 and 13.12 in *International Industrial Productivity: A Comparison of Britain, America and Germany* by A. D. Smith, D. M. W. N. Hitchens, and S. W. Davies, published by the Press Syndicate of the University of Cambridge, Cambridge, U.K., 1982.

The comparative productivity of public utilities, transportation, and communications for the U.S., U.K., and Germany are shown in Table 4.1. However, in another study, Eltis (1979, 8) reached conclusions diametrically opposite to those of Smith, Hitchens, and Davies (1982, 46). He found that the main reason for the poor performance of British public corporations was overinvestment, which was a burden on the rest of the economy.

Our empirical study of forty-six countries confirms the conclusions drawn by Pryor, by Smith, Hitchens, and Davies, by Short (1983, 27) and by others that, in the main, SOEs are engaged in capital-intensive industries. However, there are some fundamental differences between present research and earlier studies. The current research is based on a much larger sample--seventeen developed and twenty-nine developing countries. Unlike earlier studies that concentrated on one or a few sectors,

TABLE 4.2
Capital Intensity Ratio, K, for Some Developed and Developing Nations

	YEARS	$K = \frac{IP/IT}{OP/OT}$
For all 46 Countries (average)		2.26
For all 29 Developed Countries (average)		1.55
For all 17 Developing Countries (average)		2.47
Industrial Countries:		
Australia	(1954-1979)	2.00
Austria	(1970-1979)	1.27
Belgium	(1953-1979)[a]	1.35
Canada	(1970-1980)[a]	1.43
Denmark	(1974)	1.31
Finland	(1970-1975)	1.23
France	(1959-1981)	1.62
Germany	(1962-1979)[b]	1.15
Ireland	(1974-1978)[a]	1.29
Italy	(1967-1980)	2.21
Japan	(1965-1980)[a]	1.29
Netherlands	(1968-1978)[b]	3.84
Norway	(1959-1980)[a]	1.60
Spain	(1974-1980)[a]	1.54
Sweden	(1978-1980)[a]	1.59
United Kingdom	(1962-1981)	1.73
Developing Countries:		
Venezuela	(1972-1980)	1.77
Botswana	(1974-1979)	1.61
Ivory Coast	(1965-1979)[b]	2.87
Kenya	(1964-1979)	1.70
Mali	(1975-1978)	1.38
Sierra Leone	(1979)	2.57
Tanzania	(1966-1977)	2.96
Tunisia	(1967-1981)	1.36
Bangladesh	(1974)	5.44
Burma	(1968-1980)[a]	5.84
India	(1960-1978)	4.97
Korea	(1963-1980)	3.97
Pakistan	(1961-1981)	7.41

TABLE 4.2 Continued

	YEARS	$K = \frac{IP/IT}{OP/OT}$
Sri Lanka	(1961-1978)[b]	3.00
Taiwan	(1951-1980)	2.45
Thailand	(1969-1979)[b]	2.76
Greece	(1975-1979)	1.61
Malta	(1962-1980)	2.51
Portugal	(1976-1980)[b]	2.24
Turkey	(1962-1980)	3.15
Argentina	(1976-1980)	4.29
Bahamas	(1975-1980)	3.93
Barbados	(1975-1980)	1.59
Bolivia	(1971-1977)	3.60
Chile	(1974-1980)	1.17
Colombia	(1974-1980)[a]	1.45
Guyana	(1973-1980)	1.38
Mexico	(1975-1978)	3.38
Paraguay	(1970-1980)	3.61

Notes:
a: The average percentage share in GDP at factor cost (IP/IT) of industrial and developing countries was used whenever the IP/IT for the country under study was not available.
b: If IP/IT was available only for one or more than one period but not for the entire period, the available data were used as an average for capital-intensity calculation.

Source: This table is derived from "The Role of Public Enterprises: An International Statistical Comparison" in *Public Enterprises in Mixed Economies: Some Macroeconomic Aspects*, R. H. Floyd, C. S. Gray, and R. P. Short, International Monetary Fund, Washington, D.C., 1984, pp. 116-122.

this one covers the entire spectrum of SOEs. Finally, this study analyzes capital intensity and the concomitant financing aspects, but the previous research concentrated only on capital intensity.

To measure the capital intensity of an SOE, we have used the ratio of share of GFCF to share of GDP at factor cost. The capital intensity ratio, K, for all countries under investigation, as shown in Table 4.2, is above 1. The average "K" for seventeen industrial countries and twenty-nine developing countries is 1.55 and 2.47, respectively. The results of our analysis show that, compared to developed nations, the developing nations have a higher capital-intensity ratio, and both developed and developing countries have low rates of return and long pay-back periods. Given these contradictions, the existence of SOEs in developing countries is justified on two grounds: their use as a mechanism for maintaining steady economic growth and for accelerating the pace of economic development, thereby facilitating the achievement of noncommercial and macro objectives of the society. A further justification is the fact that governments have the power to socialize the economic risks by spreading the risk burden and costs over a large number of taxpayers.

The engagement of SOEs in highly capital-intensive industries may be seen as a complementary precondition and as an effective mechanism for stimulating private investment and economic growth. This, in turn, will require large amounts of financing by the state. The dependency of SOEs on external sources of finance is related to both the structural characteristics of SOEs and their obligation to respond to "socialist" objectives, such as anti-inflation, hiring redundant laborers, and rapid growth. SOEs are engaged in industries with high fixed and variable capital requirements that possess lumpy characteristics. Rapid economic growth necessitates the creation of SOEs of a certain critical size and composition in order to take advantage of economies of scale and scope. All these characteristics create financial imbalances for SOEs that, in turn, make SOEs dependent on borrowing from domestic and external sources.

Pryor (1973, 60) found that "those branches of mining and manufacturing with relatively high or low wages are roughly the same in all countries." He adds that higher wages in capital-intensive industries are due to the high proportion of skilled workers and the bargaining power of unions. For example, in the U.S., he found that the correlation between the heaviness ranking (i.e., ranking branches of manufacturing based on heavy and light criteria) and the degree of unionization, relative wages, and capital/labor ratios in 1958 were, respectively, 0.43, 0.58, and 0.41, all significant at the 0.05 level (Pryor 1973, 446). Thus, the need for financing highly capital-intensive public enterprises is further accentuated by the additional burden of higher wages in these capital-intensive industries.

The magnitudes of financial commitments are unusually large. To study the relationship between investment and financing for SOEs, we have used the simple regression analysis; multiple regression analysis was not used because, for the purpose of cross-sectional studies, the data for some key variables for many countries were not available, which would have placed a severe limitation on the scope of this study. In fact, the seemingly low values of coefficients of determination could be directly attributed to the constraints imposed by the paucity of data and an extremely limited choice of explanatory working variables. In this chapter, we have analyzed nine different relations. Equations 4.1, 4.2, and 4.3 give the results of empirical estimation of total financing (TF), domestic borrowing (DB), and foreign borrowing (FB) by SOEs, using capital intensity (K) as an explanatory variable. All endogenous variables are expressed as percentages of GDP at market prices. Y denotes the period or the closest period for which data were available. The data for the countries covered in this study are given in Appendices A4.1 through A4.9. $\bar{R}^2$ and N denote adjusted R^2 and number of countries under study, respectively. The number in parentheses denotes the standard error of coefficient.

$$TF = -0.83726 + 1.14779K \quad \bar{R}^2 = 0.46161 \qquad (4.1)$$
$$(0.37095) \quad Y = 1963\text{-}80$$
$$N = 11$$

$$DB = -1.06279 + 1.06594K \quad \bar{R}^2 = 0.32737 \qquad (4.2)$$
$$(0.32535) \quad Y = 1963\text{-}80$$
$$N = 21$$

$$FB = -0.10617 + 0.57881K \quad \bar{R}^2 = 0.16006 \qquad (4.3)$$
$$(0.24109) \quad Y = 1963\text{-}80$$
$$N = 26$$

Equation 4.1 indicates that capital intensity and total financing have a positive correlation (r=0.72, See Table 4.3) and a statistically significant regression coefficient at the 0.01 level. The regression coefficient of 1.15 indicates that a 1 percent increase in capital intensity requires a 1.15 percent increase in total financing-an elastic coefficient with respect to capital intensity. Our explanatory variable, capital intensity, accounts for 46.16 percent of the observed variation in total financing. Equation 4.1 is based

TABLE 4.3
Summary of Regression Analysis for Dependent (y) and Independent Variables and Pearson's Product Moment (r).

	Y	X	b-Co-efficient	SE	df	F Signi-ficant at	r
1.	TF	$\frac{IP/IT}{OP/OT}$	1.148	(0.371)	9	.013	.718
2.	DB	$\frac{IP/IT}{OP/OT}$	1.066	(0.325)	19	.004	.601
3.	FB	$\frac{IP/IT}{OP/OT}$	0.579	(0.241)	24	.025	.440
4.	BB_{pe}	$\frac{IP}{IT}$	0.189	(0.032)	34	.000	.714
5.	KD_{pe}	$\frac{IP}{IT}$	0.150	(0.021)	36	.000	.765
6.	D_{cg}	S_{pe}	8.480	(5.484)	11	.150	.423
7.	D_{cg}	BB_{pe}	0.487	(0.201)	42	.020	.350
8.	CG	$\frac{IP/IT}{OP/OT}$	6.659	(2.826)	11	.038	.580
9.	CP/CT	$\frac{IP/IT}{OP/OT}$	10.560	(4.955)	10	.087	.520

on eleven countries, as shown in Appendix A4.1. There are two hypotheses behind the relationship between capital intensity and total financing. First, the SOEs in most nations are more capital-intensive than their private counterparts (Shirley 1983, 13). However, this has not necessarily yielded higher profits. For instance, public corporations in the U.K. are more capital-intensive than private ones, but they generate lower surplus marketed output (See Table 6.2). The interest burden results in poor financial performance or lower surplus marketed output. A significant portion of the income of SOEs is siphoned off to pay the cost of capital formation. A comparative analysis of interest ratios in public and private enterprise in India indicated that, between 1961 and 1979, interest both as a percentage of total income and as a percentage of growth profit was higher for public enterprise. Second, the SOEs are usually involved in industries characterized by lumpiness, riskiness, and a long payback period. The involvement of SOEs in such industries is essential for social optimality. Social objectives, coupled with the involvement of SOEs in more capital-intensive industries as compared to their private counterparts, results in lower self-financing ratios for SOEs (See Chapter 3) and forces them to rely on external sources of finances. This study analyzes the capital intensity of SOEs and concomitant financing aspects; previous studies pinpointed that public enterprise deficits resulted from low productivity as a major cause of the dependency of SOEs on external sources of finance (Trivedi 1985).

Equation 4.2 demonstrates a positive correlation coefficient (r=0.60, See Table 4.3) between domestic borrowing and capital intensity. The regression coefficient shows that a 1 percent change in GFCF necessitates a 1.06 percent increase in domestic borrowing. This regression coefficient is statistically significant at the 0.0040 level. The explanatory variable accounts for 32.7 percent of the observed variation in domestic financing. Equation 4.2 is based on the twenty-one countries shown in Appendix A4.2. Equation 4.3 shows that capital intensity and foreign financing also have a positive correlation (r=0.44, See Table 4.3) and a statistically significant regression coefficient at the 0.02 level. The explanatory variable accounts for 16 percent of the observed variation in foreign financing. The regression coefficient in this equation denotes that a 1 percent increase in the explanatory variable would necessitate a 0.58 percent increase in foreign financing. Equation 4.3 is based on twenty-six countries shown in Appendix A4.3. The low magnitude of $\bar{R}^2$ indicates that there may be other explanatory variables, but the scarcity of reliable data prevented further research.

The results of regressions for the budgetary burdens (BB_{pe}) and capital account deficits (KD_{pe}) of public enterprises on their shares of GFCF (IP/IT or K^*) are given in equations 4.4 and 4.5. Equation 4.4 is derived from data of thirty-six countries as shown in Appendix A4.4. The data in equation 4.5 are derived from data of thirty-eight countries shown in Appendix A4.5.

$$BB_{pe} = -2.05200+0.18924K^{*} \quad \bar{R}^2 = 0.49610 \quad (4.4)$$
$$(0.03179) \quad Y = 1962\text{-}80$$
$$N = 36$$

$$KD_{pe} = -1.09485+0.15012K^{*} \quad \bar{R}^2 = 0.57441 \quad (4.5)$$
$$(0.02103) \quad Y = 1946\text{-}80$$
$$N = 38$$

K^{*} = IP/IT,
IP and IT = Investment of public enterprises and total investment, respectively,
BB_{pe} = Transfers and loans from governments to SOEs (as a percentage of GDP at market prices),
KD_{pe} = The part of SOEs deficit as the result of gross capital formation that is expressed as a percentage of GDP at market prices.

Equation 4.4 indicates that the investment shares of SOEs and government transfers and loans to SOEs have a positive correlation (r=0.71, See Table 4.3). This regression coefficient is statistically significant at the 0.001 percent level. The explanatory variable accounts for 50 percent of the observed variation in BB_{pe}. The regression coefficient in equation 4.4 shows that a 1 percent increase in the share of SOEs in GFCF necessitates a 0.19 percent increase in transfers and loans from government to SOEs. Equation 4.5 shows a positive correlation coefficient (r=0.77, See Table 4.3) between the share of SOEs in GFCF and their capital deficits. The explanatory variable accounts for 57 percent of the observed variation of KD_{pe}. The regression coefficient is statistically significant at the 0.001 percent level. The results of regression of central government deficits (D_{cg}) on subsidies and other current transfers from governments to SOEs (S_{pe}) is given in equation 4.6, and those of central government deficits on the budgetary burden of public enterprises in equation 4.7. Equation 4.6 is based on data from thirteen countries, as shown in Appendix A4.6, and equation 4.7 on data from forty-four countries, as shown in Appendix A4.7.

$$D_{cg} = 0.20580 + 8.4799 S_{pe} \quad \bar{R}^2 = 0.10388 \quad (4.6)$$
$$(5.48400) \quad Y = 1946\text{-}80 \quad N = 13$$

$$D_{cg} = 3.67120 + 0.48696 BB_{pe} \quad \bar{R}^2 = 0.10136 \quad (4.7)$$
$$(0.20133) \quad Y = 1946\text{-}81 \quad N = 44$$

D_{cg} = Central government deficit as a percentage of GDP at market prices,
S_{pe} = Subsidies and other current transfers of government to SOEs as a percentage of GDP at market prices.

Equation 4.6 indicates that subsidies (and other current transfers) by governments and deficits of central governments have, as expected, a positive sign (r=0.42, See Table 4.3). However, it is not significant at the 10 percent level. The explanatory variable accounts for 10 percent of the observed variation in the deficits of central governments. Equation 4.7 shows that government loans and transfers to SOEs and the deficits of central governments have a positive correlation (r=0.35, See Table 4.3) and a statistically significant regression coefficient. The explanatory variable accounts for 10 percent of the observed variation in deficits of central governments.

A cross-country regression of the growth in credit extended to SOEs as a percentage of the growth in total domestic credit (CG) and the share of SOEs in total domestic credit (CP/CT) using the capital intensity (K) as the explanatory variable are given in equations 4.8 and 4.9.

$$CG = 19.51009 + 6.65906K \quad \bar{R}^2 = 0.27497 \quad (4.8)$$
$$(2.82638) \quad Y = 1962\text{-}81 \quad N = 13$$

$$CP/CT = 10.55989 + 4.95526K \quad \bar{R}^2 = 0.19124 \quad (4.9)$$
$$(2.61124) \quad Y = 1962\text{-}81 \quad N = 12$$

Equation 4.8 indicates that capital intensity and growth in credit to SOEs have a positive correlation (r=0.58, See Table 4.3) and a statistically significant regression coefficient at the 0.05 level. Capital intensity accounts for 28 percent of the variation in growth of credit. Equation 4.8 is based on thirteen countries as shown in Appendix A4.8. Equation 4.9 demonstrates that capital intensity and share of SOEs in total domestic credit have a positive correlation (r=0.52, See Table 4.3) and a statistically significant regression coefficient at the 10 percent level. Capital intensity accounts for 0.20 percent of the variation in the share of SOEs in total domestic credit. Equation 4.9 is based on twelve countries, as shown in Appendix A4.9.

Conclusion

In Chapters 1 and 3, it is shown that SOEs are engaged in capital-intensive industries. Therefore, it appears that those economists who have emphasized that the main reasons for establishing SOEs are political and historical have ignored the fact that many of these enterprises, in order to meet urgent social needs, had to be undertaken by governments because private enterprise simply was not forthcoming, due to extremely heavy initial investments and uncertain returns. This, coupled with relatively higher wages in such industries, gives rise to the dependency of SOEs on either domestic or foreign sources of finance. From our analysis, we can now confirm the hypothesis that these conditions do contribute to the overall deficits of public enterprises. This analysis further shows that the deficits of SOEs make a relatively small contribution to the overall deficits of various governments and, hence, cannot be used as an explanation for the deficits of the central governments. The results of our analysis are summarized in Table 4.3.

5

Price Formation for SOEs

In this chapter, we shall investigate whether it would be appropriate to apply the pricing policies suggested by welfare economists to SOEs. The factors and restrictions that prevent us from using these policies will also be explored. It will be shown that there is a need for alternative policies based on a more realistic axiom of cost of production. This approach will allow us to concentrate on costs, rather than rely on often fictitious estimates of demand and welfare embodying such concepts as consumer surplus.

Pricing, finance, and investment are interrelated factors. Regardless of the type of ownership, the key difference in pricing decisions is whether such interrelated decisions are made internally or externally. In the private sector, they are made internally, but in the case of SOEs, such decisions, more often than not, are made externally. Since SOEs have a mixture of commercial and social objectives in their pricing decisions, as Bös (1981, 123) points out, the influence of social and political factors cannot be ignored:

> In my opinion the most commonly presented economic reasoning (the economies of scale argument, the external effects argument, the public goods argument, the anti-profit [pro-welfare] argument etc.) is not very convincing. Thus in my opinion, it is primarily for political reasons that goods are produced publicly and therefore a political theory seems to be the best way to explain the problem.

Consequently, the differences in the characteristics of private enterprises and those of SOEs prevent us from codifying a single pricing policy for both, especially when there are vast differences among the SOEs themselves. In the last decade, there has been a tremendous change in the goals set for SOEs in the U.K., France, Sweden, and other countries. Changes in their goals and policies were necessitated by poor pricing policies implemented over a long period of time. The failure to achieve the targets set by governments and the financial crises faced by SOEs have forced governments to place more emphasis on commercial objectives and, in some cases, even to seek profits. For instance, when we look at the different policies in the U.K. from 1960 to the present, we find that such changes have taken place gradually for political purposes. The problems of unmet financial targets, external financing limits, and more privatization can all be explained by a simple statement, that is, although SOEs may have price structure problems, they also have price structure opportunities (Nelson 1976, 55).

External financing limits may be interpreted in several ways, such as a cut in both costs and level of unprofitable activities or an improved productivity in commercial and noncommercial functions. If none of these ways is explicitly specified, this could be interpreted as giving more autonomy to SOEs so that they may raise prices and meet their financing needs. This increase in prices would be facilitated whenever SOEs have monopoly power. Posner concluded that the government could use SOEs as "surrogate indirect tax raisers," especially those that were engaged in monopoly enterprise (Posner, quoted in Redwood and Hatch 1982, 96). Setting a target rate of return subject to imposed social objectives is merely another way of saying that SOEs should run commercially. The extent of SOEs' commercialization and their pricing policies depend on what these enterprises are being called upon to do. Their economic circumstances are highly dependent upon the competitive environment in which they operate. It is not feasible to establish a general pricing formula that could be used for all SOEs. For instance, as pointed out by Munby and others, the long-run marginal cost (LRMC) is not really a "general" rule. Rather, it is a "specific" rule, applicable only under carefully specified conditions. Regarding this subject, Munby has this to say (Munby, quoted in Tivey, 1973, 99):

> Pricing policies are too complicated to be codified in the form of a simple criterion, such as long run marginal cost which is likely to become more of a slogan than a rational guide to economic policy.

Nancy Ruggles (1968, 126) takes the same position:

> No one formula can be established which will be valid as a general principle. But one statement can be made: the search for a panacea, for a single simple rule by which to guide all conduct, is, because of technological requirements of the dif-

ferent parts of the economy and because of the problems of redistribution, a vain search and even a foolish one.

We do not use the term "general" in the same sense as Ruggles does. "General formula" is used by us merely as a guideline, subject to specific conditions and circumstances for each SOE. From our point of view, we do not suggest the use of a single simple rule. The term "general formula" will be used as a center of gravity for price formation, subject to certain imposed constraints. In other words, pricing policies for each SOE may be tailored on the basis of this more general formula. In the rest of this chapter, we shall discuss some of the problems involved in marginal cost pricing (MCP) and review some empirical evidence that reveals the need for alternative pricing formulas based on more realistic theoretical foundations.

Marginal Cost Pricing

The microeconomic theory argument concerning pricing in SOEs revolves around the optimal allocation of resources and welfare maximization. Welfare economists believe that the utilization of MCP would place society on its welfare frontier, and on this frontier, all Pareto optimality conditions would be satisfied. Henderson and Quandt (1971, 280) write that "a social welfare function is an ordinal index of society's welfare and is a function of the utility levels of all individuals." The supporters of MCP assume that utility is measurable, a view similar to that of nineteenth-century economists, such as Jevons, Walras, and Marshall. The concept of consumer surplus is used for measuring the utility of an individual. It is the difference between how much the consumer is willing to pay and his or her actual payment. Consumer surplus is the net benefit derived from consumption, and it should, at best, be viewed as only a suggestive approximation because the consumer may not reveal his true willingness to pay. Some economists, such as Varian (1978, 92) and Bös (1981, Chapter 1) in their analysis of consumer surplus, prefer Marshallian demand (an ordinary demand function) to Hicksian demand (a compensated demand function) since the latter is based on unobservable utility functions and the former is based on price and income data. Estimating consumer surplus is even more complicated and less realistic whenever there is more than one good. For this reason, consumer surplus is often studied in partial equilibrium analysis by assuming that variation in other prices is small, and, consequently, the income effect may be safely ignored. The significance of consumer surplus depends upon whether changes in prices occur in a stepwise fashion or all at once. We believe MCP is neither free from all practical problems of cost benefit analysis nor based on unrestrictive assumptions.

Among the economists who advocate the use of marginal analysis in order to maximize welfare, we may mention Pigou, Wicksell, Pareto, Barone, Harrod, Hotelling, and Bergson. This trend of thought has dominated most of the guidelines for practical advice on a pricing system for SOEs. For instance, Meade (1944) strongly recommends that MCP be applied to the pricing policies of SOEs. Boiteux (1971) and Masse (1962) in France and Turvey (1971) in England are among economists who believe that MCP should be utilized. Hartley (1977, 30) believes MCP is appropriate for both private and nationalized industries. Samuelson, Arrow, and Lange argue that the satisfaction of marginality conditions does not necessarily mean the provision of an absolute maximum in welfare, but only a relative maximum (Ruggles 1968, 30-31). Any point on the Grand Utility Possibility Frontier (GUPF) may be regarded as a relative maximum, except that the tangency of the GUPF and an indifference curve (i.e., the bliss point) does yield maximum welfare in absolute terms. Samuelson states that the satisfaction of Pareto optimality conditions (i.e., satisfaction of all the marginality conditions) fails to consider the question of income distribution. Thus, Pareto optimality is a weak condition for welfare maximization. If all other things were equal, then the pricing system that satisfies the marginality conditions would also provide a greater welfare when compared with prices that do not satisfy marginality conditions. In this assertion, Samuelson, Arrow, and Lange differ from Pigou, Wicksell, Pareto, and Barone in that the latter believe the satisfaction of marginality conditions would bring maximum welfare in absolute terms, not merely in relative terms (Ruggles 1968, 30-31).

If the employment of the optimal amount of factors of production or optimal plant size is assumed, then both short-term and long-term marginal costs will be equal (Bös 1981, 29). If the MCP has any value at all, it should rely on long-term estimates rather than short-term ones. This statement is based on the nature of costs and periodic fluctuations in demand encountered by most SOEs. Capacity utilization in most industries, such as electricity, telephone, airports, and other types of transportation, is highly variable. This makes long-term pricing formation more realistic than short-term policies. The involvement of SOEs in substantially capital-intensive and expensive industries with high financial requirements for expansion and growth necessitates their concentration on joint products and setting of their prices based on long-term cost estimates. One major objection to the LRMC approach is the difficulty of translating it into an operational method.

The interdependency among pricing, financing, and investment and the consequences of such interdependency on the rest of the economy make long-term perspectives even more realistic. In the case of increasing returns to scale, the application of MCP to regulated industries would result in deficits. Financing these deficits by means of taxation would affect other variables in the system, such as the labor market, private investment, and income distribution. The use of taxation for financing deficits cannot be considered "distributionally neutral," and it may interfere with the optimal allocation of resources. This conflicts with the original objective of MCP. Ramsey's price and the three Bs'--Baumol, Bradford, and Boiteux--approaches are discussed in the following section. Their approaches are based on MCP, and all rely on the inverse elasticities of demand in order to avoid deficits and cover their costs. Therefore, their pricing procedures are dependent upon the relevant price and cross-elasticities (Bös 1981, 95). Both of these elasticities are subject to serious estimation problems.

Marginal Cost Pricing: Controversies

Marginal cost pricing is an incomplete and imperfect guideline for decisionmaking in SOEs, and the following criticisms may be made. This pricing guideline is based on a number of explicit and implicit assumptions: the marginal utility of income is held constant (the original Pigouvian assumption), the factors of production are fixed, and the use of some type of taxation to cover any losses caused by MCP will not affect the optimal allocation of the factors of production (Rees 1968, 260). Increases in output are considered to be the same as increases in welfare, without considering possible changes in the distribution of income (Ruggles 1968). These assumptions are too unrealistic for practical use in the real world.

First, in welfare economics, it is assumed that a rational consumer has diminishing marginal utility. Income, like leisure, is a source of utility. Pfouts (1960, 113-132) considers income to be simply another type of good. Gould and Lazear (1989, 112) have followed his approach. If we follow this argument, then the marginal utility of income cannot be held constant. Second, if taxes are used to finance the deficits of SOEs, this will affect the supply of productive factors. Third, MCP is very unrealistic in an economy with imperfect markets. As already stated, the equality of price to marginal cost would not be met unless government regulation has already been imposed. If an industry is obligated to follow government regulations, the source of funding needed to cover their losses should be specified beforehand. Finally, SOEs normally do not follow the doctrine of MCP, and they may very well be obligated to achieve a target rate of return.

Among the reasons for applying MCP are the satisfaction of Pareto optimality conditions and improving the welfare of the members of society. Although MCP remains the primary concern of general equilibrium theory; nonetheless, if the Lerner-Lange rule concerning MCP is applied to only one segment of the economy, such as SOEs, it will not guarantee an optimum efficient allocation of resources in all other sectors, unless the marginality conditions have also been sustained between and within all sectors of the entire economy. If such is the case, Bös (1981, 71) suggests the substitution of general equilibrium theory by the theory of second-best:

> Consider publicly supplied goods that are sold at marginal cost prices, and substitutional or complementary privately supplied good that are priced above marginal costs. It can be shown that in such a case welfare in general can be increased if the public enterprise sets prices deviating from marginal costs (second-best prices).

Furthermore, Norris (1947, 54-62) and Little (1957, 214) have emphasized that there are serious problems with the identification and measurement of marginal cost. Therefore, a highly sophisticated model is needed to solve these problems. For this reason, the average costs of increasing production are used as a proxy for marginal costs. This approximation cannot be considered a reliable means of cost estimation because it may not embody all the costs of production (Little 1957, 40-41). Since costs of SOEs are studied over a relatively long time interval, it is more accurate to utilize the changes in the combination of both direct and indirect costs as a proxy for marginal costs, if they are applicable at all. The issue of identification and measurement becomes even more serious in cases where factors of production are used in joint products. SOEs are highly involved in joint production, such as transportation services, postal services, telecommunications, and electricity. The outputs of these enterprises may at different times satisfy entirely different needs.

Many SOEs are engaged in the production of periodical output. Consequently, marginal costs will be different for peak and off-peak time. The efficient allocation of resources would be achieved only when the equality of price and marginal costs is satisfied during all periods. Thus, costs are closely related to time, and time actually changes the characteristics of goods and services. Kahn (1970, 71), among other economists, believes that price should incorporate all costs attributable to production of an additional unit, regardless of when the costs are actually incurred. We believe that if Kahn's position is accepted, ex-ante pricing guidelines based on marginal costs would not be useful because changes that take place in a dynamic world would also influence other variables in the system. In Chapter 2, it was pointed out that most SOEs are engaged in highly capital-intensive industries with lumpiness and indivisibility characteristics. MCP, on the other hand, is based on the divisibility of assets. Thus, the indivisibility characteristics of the SOEs' assets violate the first order condition for Pareto optimality.

SOEs usually are engaged in multiplant activities, e.g., electricity. Each plant in the system does not necessarily operate with the same techniques of production, due to the age of the establishment, the time of takeover, different operating costs, and other factors. This heterogeneity within the system prevents us from deriving a unique standard for pricing policy because different marginal costs create different Pareto optimality conditions. Some economists, such as Wilson (1945) and Coase (1946), agree that MCP would not serve as a basis for proper guidelines for investment decisions. Vickrey (1948) points out that this problem is caused by the decreasing cost structure of the given industry, not by the concept of MCP itself. Inefficiency is not eliminated by MCP because all factors must be considered--namely, profits, prices, and costs. If we consider only the case where costs are arbitrarily manipulated, then neither allocative nor X-efficiency would be guaranteed by the application of MCP (Nelson 1976, 62).

The claimed social welfare gains from MCP are based on a presupposed "ideal" distribution of income. If, for financing deficits, the pricing system is combined with general taxes, it affects the original ideal income distribution. Thus, the use of taxation for financing deficits cannot be considered distributionally neutral, and it may interfere with the optimal allocation of resources. Some economists, such as Hotelling and Henderson, believe that the distributional effects of this policy are negligible, but others, including Coase, disagree (Little 1957, 186-188). We believe that if the ex-ante income distribution is ideal, the ex-post will not be, especially when people in the higher brackets of income pay more taxes (assuming that taxation is based on the principle of ability to pay) and receive fewer benefits for their contributions. This criticism is based on the lack of equality of treatment by the government, rather than whether the ex-post income distribution is superior or inferior to the ex-ante one. Whenever MCP is studied in conjunction with the necessary taxation or other forms of financing, it is impossible to continue the analysis in an objective and accurate manner without becoming involved in the problem of making interpersonal comparisons between losers and gainers. Ruggles (1968, 25) argues that:

> It is not possible to design a pricing system upon the basis of some criterion of efficiency, and then to alter income distribution in any desired way without affecting the efficiency of the pricing system. No such separation of the problem is possible.

Bös (1981, 44), in regard to distributional consequences of MCP, writes:

> In the case of decreasing ray average costs the comparatively low price level may be distributionally positive if the publicly supplied goods are mainly consumed by low-income earners. But if according to the first-best allocation theory the public deficits are financed by lump sum taxes the regressive impact of these taxes may compensate the above mentioned positive effects.

Shepherd (1976a, 133), in writing on the fairness of MCP, has taken the following position:

> Efficient price structures strictly in line with marginal costs may violate fairness, in some cases quite sharply. Therefore a rush toward marginal costs pricing might in fact burden rate structures with more discrimination and unfairness than the optimists expect.

We believe that MCP is an incomplete pricing system, unless the source of financing deficits is identified. Some advocates of MCP, such as Lerner, Meade, Troxel, Reder, Vickrey, Hotelling, and Samuelson, either ignore the sources of subsidies for financing deficits or offer proposals for financing them that contradict or depart from the marginality conditions (Ruggles 1968, 31-33). Some of the proposals by the advocates of MCP are discussed below.

Hotelling (1938, 242-269), among others, suggests the use of lump sum taxes, because he believes they do not violate the marginality conditions.

He suggests using such taxes on the site value of land, inheritance, commodities in limited supply, or income. Income taxes could fall into a lump sum category if and only if the supply of labor is assumed to be perfectly inelastic; otherwise, they would affect the choice between work and leisure that would again violate our original marginality conditions (Samuelson 1948, 240). This effect of taxes on the supply of the factors of production has to be considered in a general equilibrium model. Changes in the supply of factors of production will depend upon the actual incidence of these taxes. We believe that if a lump sum tax is imposed on income, in the long run there would be a change in work-leisure preferences and changes in consumption, savings, and investment. Little (1957, 187) argues that "lump sum taxes are neither ordinary, nor practical." In the same regard, Arrow (1981, 64) writes:

> If the first-best optimum involves some losses to enterprises, the losses should be made up through taxation, but we are not concerned about the details. Ramsey and Lintner argue that the money has to come from somewhere; there is no such thing as a lump sum tax. Taxes have to be imposed on some economic behavior. Any tax is essentially an excise tax—that abomination of the welfare economist.

If the financing of deficits is taken into account, MCP would never be a first-best. Frisch (1939) is among the advocates of a second approach, where prices would be proportional to marginal costs. This violates marginality conditions (i.e., MRS≠ MRTS), unless the return to the factors of production increases with the same markup as marginal costs. Frisch's proposal also faces the problem of identifying the necessary incremental changes in both marginal costs and marginal product. This problem becomes insurmountable in the production of joint products.

Still a third proposal for covering these deficits is the application of price discrimination. In this approach, marginality conditions would not be violated since the consumer faces the same set of prices at the margin, but pays different prices for intramarginal units (Webb 1976b, 73). This approach is complex, inequitable, and costly. It charges inequitable prices to different consumers and requires perfect knowledge of the demand elasticity, as well as cross-elasticity. The high administrative costs of this approach might also create X-inefficiency in production (Leibenstein 1978, 162). The final proposal is the use of the three Bs' approach or Ramsey prices, based on the theory of second-best. This approach was first explored by Ramsey in 1927 and revised in the early 1970s by Baumol and Bradford (1970) and Boiteux (1981). In this approach, the cross-price elasticities are assumed to be approximately zero because they are very small compared with direct ones. In other words, if the firm is engaged in the provision of different services, demand curves are assumed to be independent of each other. The lowest price is based on marginal cost, and any increase above marginal cost must be inversely proportional to the elasticity of demand. Prices would increase the least (most) for consumers with the most (least) elastic demand. The supporters of the three Bs' approach argue that it is superior to alternative approaches because total costs are covered with the least degree of inefficiency. Their approach does not distort the supply of labor and capital and produces only a small distortion in the optimal consumption pattern. We believe that the three Bs' approach has a limited applicability because it ignores the problems involved in the estimation of elasticities. If the assumption of zero cross-elasticities is made, the model is inadequate to explore the joint product characteristics so often found in SOEs. The Ramsey formula (Bös 1981, 57) for only two goods may be shown by the following equation:

$$\frac{\Delta P_i}{\Delta P_j} = \frac{E_{jj} - E_{ij}}{E_{ii} - E_{ji}} \tag{5.1}$$

$$\Delta P_i = \frac{P_i - C_i}{P_i} \tag{5.2}$$

E_{ij} (or E_{ji}) and E_{ii} (or E_{jj}) = Cross-price elasticity and their own price elasticity, respectively,
ΔP_i = Price-cost margin,
$i = 1,2,$
$j = 1,2.$

If the cross-price elasticity is equal to zero, then the ratio of the price-cost margin is equal to the inverse elasticities of demand. This system of pricing requires a thorough knowledge of both price and cross-elasticities of demand. Ramsey prices may be criticized on the grounds that they contradict the equal treatment of individuals by SOEs and may not be distributionally neutral or nondiscriminatory. This pricing procedure might also result in higher prices for inelastic necessities that are a part of the everyday consumption of poor people.

In practice, there are problems associated with cost classification and specification. For example, which costs should be classified as constant or variable? MCP is based on historical cost, not replacement cost. If replacement cost is greater than historical cost, then pricing based on marginal cost will underestimate the true cost of production. The use of the doctrine of MCP not only faces severe administrative difficulties it also involves substantial costs for monitoring its practical application. Furthermore, the concept itself is ambiguous, and there is some question about its workability and practicality. Melody (1976, 205), in commenting upon the implementation of MCP for utilities, takes the following position:

> I strongly disagree with Shepherd's assessment of contributions of marginal cost pricing. Whereas he appears to rank this first, I would place it last. Where he ranks it as a positive benefit, I would consider it perhaps the greatest detriment. I do so because marginal cost pricing, in my observation of its application, simply has provided a glossy rationale for the preservation of infinite pricing flexibility for utility management. In the name of theoretical precision, marginal cost provides infinite costing flexibility to justify the infinite pricing flexibility desired by every monopolist. The deficiencies of marginal cost in both theory and practice make it essentially unworkable as an objective standard for management or for regulation.

Joskow (1976, 200) agrees that:

> All things considered, the contributions of American, British and French economists indicate that the application of marginal cost pricing principles to actual calculation of prices is considerably more complicated than simple prescriptions. Considerations of demand elasticity, uncertainty, rationing costs, heterogenous technology, and other complications of actual systems can help to extend the basic principles to incorporate additional considerations that more accurately reflect reality.

Little (1957, 194) also supports this line of argument, noting that "the general case against marginal-cost pricing is clearly overwhelming. All the arguments, are against it."

Marginal Cost Pricing: Empirical Evidence

First, we will investigate the extent to which MCP has been recommended as a pricing policy for SOEs in the U.K. Later, we will discuss the actual application of these pricing guidelines to some of the SOEs in the U.K. and other countries. No guidelines for pricing policy on SOEs were given in the U.K.'s 1961 White Paper, but the 1967 White Paper contains very comprehensive ones and explicitly identifies the features and principles that underlie their relationships to the government. The main guidelines in the 1967 White Paper (i.e., Treasury) are as follows:

> ...Nationalized industries' revenues should normally cover their accounting costs in full (Paragraph 17).
>
> ...Pricing policies should be devised with reference to the costs of the particular goods and services provided. Unless this is done, there is a risk of undesirable cross-subsidization and consequent misallocation of resources (Paragraph 18).
>
> ...In addition to recovering accounting costs, prices need to be reasonably related to costs at the margin and to be designed to promote the efficient use of resources within an industry. Where there is spare capacity...or excess demand, short-run marginal costs are revelvant. In the long run, the main consideration is the cost of supplying on a continuing basis (i.e., long-run marginal costs)(Paragraph 21).

From the 1967 White Paper, it is clear that SOEs were explicitly urged to adopt MCP, and whenever possible cross-subsidization was to be avoided. Thus, the MCP was designed to maximize allocative efficiency for given demand. Molyneux and Thompson (1987) document numerous examples where the 1967 White Paper guidelines were simply ignored. A study conducted by Coopers and Lybrand Associates (CLA, 1976) concentrated on four SOEs--the British Gas Corporation, the British Railway Boards, the British Steel Corporation, and the Post Office Telecommunication. The CLA, after investigating the pricing policies of these four SOEs, concluded that "none of the four nationalized industries currently based their pricing policies on either long-run or short-run marginal cost" (CLA 1976, 100). For instance, the Post Office Telecommunication and British Gas all set their prices on a cost-plus basis, with the "plus" reflecting their current financial objectives. According to the CLA report, financial targets and sociopolitical objectives of SOEs were the main factors in their pricing policies.

In the 1978 White Paper, no specific guidelines or strategies were given for price formation. However, in the 1967 White Paper, the guidelines explicitly stated that SOEs should adopt MCP. The omission of MCP from the more recent guidelines may be attributed to two factors: the inapplicability and complexities of MCP and the conflict between MCP and financial targets. The 1978 White Paper introduced, in lieu of precise guidelines, an "open strategy" for pricing. The details of the pricing structure were to be determined by SOEs in conjunction with their market circumstances and in light of their overall objectives, including financial goals. Imposing financial targets and requiring the SOEs to cover their full costs, including the opportunity cost of their capital, created a pricing structure similar to that of traditional economics. To achieve their financial objectives and the RRR, SOEs had to base their prices on average costs with a specified markup. The possibility of markup pricing with some degree of price discrimination should be expected whenever financial targets are imposed. The markup would depend on the expected rate of return and whether the SOEs were obligated to finance the cost of governmentally imposed objectives. Bates and Fraser (1974, 82-86) argue that if the SOEs had any doubt about reaching their financial objectives they would adopt one or more of the following options: raise their prices, cut investments, or use a faster rate of depreciation that would reduce their net assets. They believe that SOEs have used their financial goals first and foremost as a pricing criteria.

From this discussion, it follows that imposition of financial constraints encourages SOEs to adopt more traditional pricing methods. This may have led the SOEs away from an efficient allocation of resources because in this instance financial viability became the central issue, not the satisfaction of the Pareto optimality condition. Keyser, Windle, and Stares (1978, 141) pointed out that in England after 1974, when price restraint policies were abolished, the SOEs returned to "more economic pricing policies," such as average cost pricing. The evidence against the use of MCP is also found in some other countries. For instance, in France in 1958, *Electricite de France* applied a uniform markup pricing policy to cover a 4 percent deficit. Keyser, Windle, and Stares (1978, 144) point out that in the Federal Republic of Germany post office prices are based on what the market will bear. Their studies also show that cross-subsidization in EEC countries between and within industries has been practiced.

The right pricing model is crucial for the long-term survival of SOEs. Adopting wrong pricing policies may result in changes in the quality of goods and services, shifts in ownership, higher taxes, or the use of alternative sources of finance, such as cross-subsidization. At least one, and in most cases a combination, has been implemented in most countries during recent years. Policy implementation depends upon political acceptability and sensitivity, as well as economic conditions. A number of governments, including the U.K., Italy, Sweden, Republic of Korea, and Brazil, are in the process of divestiture or have already divested some of their SOEs. The high capital requirements, fears of nationalization, and the attempts of governments to unload their losses have made this process of privatization very difficult. In some cases, the NCOs of SOEs are so important that divestiture seems impossible. Thus, the sale of SOEs to the domestic private sector or passing of legislation to force SOEs to act more like private enterprises, by using profit as a watchword, is not uncommon in many countries, especially in the EEC countries. The speed of privatization is influenced by the political climate and the growth of deficits of both SOEs and the central government.

In discussing pricing models, there are a number of questions that need to be answered. What is the specific goal of the government in establishing a given SOE? In what kind of market does the SOE operate, and what are its technological requirements? What kinds of goods and services are produced by the SOEs, e.g., necessities or luxuries? Are pricing decisions external or internal to the given SOEs? What kinds of costs are to be covered by the pricing policies? All these questions have been dealt with in the body of this chapter.

Pricing Mechanism: Cost-Axiomatic

Problems associated with the pricing policies suggested by welfare economists require that they be based on more realistic axioms, such as the cost of production. This approach allows us to concentrate on measurable variables (i.e., costs), rather than on fictitious estimates of elasticities of demand and welfare that usually embody such concepts as consumer surplus and utility functions. Some economists, such as Bös and Tillman (1981, 116), have expressed fears that MCP procedure may even result in welfare minimization. According to a study by Brown and Heal (1980), MCP does not necessarily satisfy Pareto optimality conditions.

The survival of SOEs requires an accurate estimation of the costs of production. Prices should be fair for both the SOEs and the consumers of their products. Therefore, prices will be fair if they are properly based on the true costs of production. If markup pricing is adopted, it must be based on full costs, not merely prime costs. Levine (1981, 84) includes both prime and overhead costs, whereas Kalecki (1969) includes only prime costs in his cost-plus pricing policy. In the full-cost pricing model, the "true cost pricing system", pricing is based on a combination of prime and overhead costs. This pricing model incorporates all the costs that are involved in the entire production process. Cost classification should be based on fixed costs (e.g., indirect, overhead, or supplementary costs) and variables costs (e.g., direct, prime, running, and operating costs). Fixed costs refer to total financial obligations that are independent of production and capacity usage. Indirect costs are fixed only for a short period of time. The true estimation of overhead costs should include both explicit and implicit ones. Taking into account only the former costs may underestimate the true costs of production and overestimate the performance of SOEs. The estimation of overhead costs is more complicated for those SOEs that are involved in joint production and where there are both "economies of scale" and "economies of scope." Economies of scale are related to changes in the magnitude of costs as a result of a rise or fall in production, and economies of scope explain the fluctuations in outlays due to a change in the composition of output. Issues related to these economies will be studied later in this chapter.

An accurate classification and allocation of overhead costs should lead to a better understanding of cost and ultimately of price formation. An accurate allocation of overhead costs occurs when the estimation of the technical coefficients for each input in the entire specific line of production is possible. Although this may be difficult in practice, one could use the "single product technique" suggested by Baumol, Panzar, and Willig (1982, 446) to estimate the overhead costs of joint products. In this method, different outputs are crystallized into a single measure called the scalar output. Semmler (1984, 160-185) demonstrates how the system of joint production could be transformed into a single product system with multiple activities. If the SOEs are engaged in joint production with nonseparable activities, their alternative cost allocations could be based on either some value weights or some physical characteristics of their outputs measured in quantitative units.

We know that many SOEs utilize highly expensive inputs that might necessitate their concentration in joint products in order to use both economies of scope and scale. When this is the case, the SOEs could use, with suitable modifications, the procedures widely employed by private enterprises for estimating cost shares for decomposed joint products. These procedures can, however, be used only if it is assumed that the particular SOEs are not obligated to meet any NCOs. One of the most commonly used methods in cost accounting, the "decomposition technique," is based on market value (share value or sale value). In this method, joint products are decomposed into multiple products. If decomposed outputs are marketable and marketed, the costs are based on proportion of their sales value. This method has been used by private enterprise since Marshall first introduced it in 1890 (Semmler 1984, 171-187). One indirect and external procedure for estimating sales value is based on a comparison with another enterprise that produces a single product. The accuracy of such indirect estimation may be improved if the comparison were made with an industry that has similar input intensity. This indirect estimation of overhead costs is then used as a proxy guideline for cost efficiency in those SOEs that produce joint products. It is expected that such SOEs will be more cost efficient because of both economies of scale and economies of scope.

When SOEs have a mixture of commercial objectives and NCOs, the SOEs must be compensated for their social objectives in accordance with the "contract plan." If the separation of commercial and noncommercial costs is possible and consumers are not directly charged for any portion of the costs of meeting NCOs, the sales value method might be applied. When SOEs operate in an oligopolistic framework, the accuracy of the sales value method can be improved by using an adjusted average production price based on the experience of all other producers who are not obligated to meet NCOs. The use of average prices is more accurate because exchange of commodities takes place at average prices (Semmler 1985, 258-278). Adjusted average price refers to an average price that does not include average markup.

Another approach for estimating the cost of joint products uses a concept called the "condensed factor." This is a mixture of physical units and assigned weights, where the latter are related to social desirability and social necessity. This mixture of quantitative and qualitative factors transforms all the joint products into a unique measurement system. Even if the outputs of joint products could be measured in terms of a single unit, such as tons, miles, etc., cost accounting based solely on these physical units may still be biased. For instance, the volume of different categories of mail could not be used as a basis for measuring cost shares because we cannot average out heterogenous products. The position taken by Semmler (1984, 177) in regard to the use of physical units as a basis for allocating the cost of joint products is that such a measure may be applicable in certain cases and not in others. When the cost sharing is based on the "condensed factor," the accuracy of the assigned weight plays a critical role. The weight describes the condensed form of all variables except quantity. Although the inclusion of this "hedonic variable," which is a mixture of various objectives, introduces some element of subjectivity into this method, it is still preferable to other approaches that use average unit cost or weighted averages. In the weighted average method, the cost of each joint product is based on the weighted expected market value. The hedonic variable in the condensed factor approach is weighted for a mixture of objectives, rather than the expected market value. The magnitude of this hedonic variable for SOEs will depend upon social objectives and the assigned social values for each objective.

The overhead costs are defined by Levine (1981, 81) as "the sum of the expenses incurred in constituting the firm as a producing and marketing potential makes up its overhead costs." Based on Levine's definition, the following costs should be included in overhead costs: depreciation, interest paid on productive inputs, wages and salaries of labor and management that are necessary for sustaining the institutional structure of the firm, and circulating capital that is consumed in maintaining the productive potential of the unit of capital. The true estimation of overhead costs should include the implicit cost of capital whenever investment is not financed by borrowing, e.g., investment from surplus. The average supplementary cost may be written as equation 5.3.

$$ASC = \frac{D_r + W_n + S_n + K_b + K_i + M}{(ARC)(MD)} = \frac{TSC}{Z} \qquad (5.3)$$

TSC = Total supplementary costs,
ASC = Average supplementary costs for the forecast level of capacity utilization,
D_r = Depreciation at replacement costs,
W_n = Wages of necessary labor,
S_n = Salaries of necessary management,

K_b = Interest paid on borrowed capital,
K_i = Implicit interest on capital,
M = Cost of material for keeping the fixed capital in operation,
ARC = Available rate of capacity, which is the average capacity utilization if SOEs have multiplant operations,
MD = Market demand for SOEs output at each period of time,
Z = Forecast rate of SOEs sales.

Operating costs are defined by Levine (1981, 82): "The cost incurred in the transformation of the firm's economic potential into a stream of commodity products are the prime costs associated directly with the production of the individual units of product." Obviously, the magnitude of operating costs over a period of time depends on the costs of their components, the technical coefficients between and within inputs, and the total output. In the use of operating costs, including the following components is necessary: the quantity and price of the necessary materials and the total wage bill paid for the necessary labor. Levine (1981, 83) further divides labor costs into two main components, namely, prime and overhead costs. According to this breakdown, those labor costs that are incurred in the process of transformation into individual products are a part of prime costs, and those that are used to maintain the unit of capital are a component of overhead costs. The total operating cost may be written as equation 5.4.

$$TOC = \sum_{i=1}^{s} K_i + \sum_{i=1}^{n} W_i L_i + \sum_{i=1}^{k} m_i M_i \tag{5.4}$$

$$UOC = \frac{TOC}{MD}$$

TOC = Total operating costs,
UOC = Unit operating costs,
MD = Market demand,
K_i = Expenses of capital in direct production,
W_i = Wage paid to laborer in direct production,
L_i = Laborer employed in direct production,
W_iL_i = Total wage bill in direct production,
m_i = Material used in direct production,

M_i = Cost for a unit of materials used in production,
m_iM_i = Total cost of materials used in direct production,
$i = 1,...,n$ = Number of heterogenous laborers in direct production,
$i = 1,...,k$ = Number of heterogenous materials in direct production,
$i = 1,...,s$ = Number of different kinds of capital.

Pricing Policies: Post-Keynesian and Post-Marxian

We have thus far discussed financing, pricing, and investment as interrelated factors. In recent years, there has been a change in government behavior with regard to their expectations from SOEs. In England, Sweden, France, and other countries, there have been attempts to run SOEs to some extent as commercial entities. In most of these countries, there is a preset target rate of return for many of the SOEs that is set differently for each industry. In any pricing model, high capital/output ratios are inseparable from a high proportion of fixed capital in industries, and, therefore, markup and target rates of return are necessary for the reproduction, expansion, and control of large amounts of fixed capital. We have stated that a general pricing model based on cost-plus pricing may be used for SOEs. The "plus" here refers to the target rate of return that is preset by decisionmakers and may embody different objectives. This model rests upon two premises, namely, that prices are not based on marginal costs and that the recommended pricing model does not conflict with the pricing policies of SOEs. Pricing with a target rate of return is similar to Semmler's (1984) pricing policies of modern large corporations that are based on cost-plus a margin. These pricing policies are similar to Brody's markup pricing policies for socialist planning (Brody, quoted in Semmler 1984, 163). The size of markup or target rate of return will depend upon what specific objectives are expected to be met from the preset target rate of return.

Internal financing and/or accumulation of surplus for growth, expansion, entry into new industrial ventures, cross-subsidization, or financing of NCOs–any one or more of these could be such an objective. If markup pricing is being used as a source of financing, the potential loss of sales that may result from higher markups must be considered a part of implicit costs. SOEs may be divided into two categories: those that have no NCOs and those that have a mixture of commercial objectives and NCOs. Naturally, pricing models for the two categories must be different. Under Case I below, we discuss the models developed for SOEs with no NCOs, and in Case II, we take up the discussion of pricing models related to SOEs with a mixture of commercial objectives and NCOs.

Case I

The markup pricing or target rates of return may also be used as a measure of performance evaluation for enterprises with high capital-intensive ratios whenever SOEs are not obligated to perform any social objectives. In those cases where SOEs have no NCOs and use multiplant production for a single product, markup pricing is described in the following formulation, designed by us and based on Semmler's work (1984):

$$P = UOC + ASC + r(K/Z) = UOC(1+\mu) \qquad (5.5)$$

P = Price per unit,
UOC = Operating cost per unit,
ASC = Average supplementary costs,
r = Target rate of return,
K = Capital advanced (fixed and circulating),
Z = Forecast rate of output sale,
μ = Markup factor.

Equation 5.5 is shown graphically in Figure 5.1. The cost and prices are shown on the vertical axis, and the degree of capacity utilization along the horizontal axis. The price that the consumer pays is shown as a negative function of capacity utilization because the average fixed cost decreases as capacity utilization increases. But once the stage of a 100 percent capacity utilization is reached, any further increase in demand can be met only by creating additional capacity, which, in turn, will result in an increase in price.

In Figure 5.1, once the rate of capacity utilization has been estimated, the price becomes determinate because costs, markups, and the target rate of return are all fixed for that particular level of capacity utilization. If the rate of capacity utilization is overestimated, the resulting prices will not be sufficient to meet all costs and, therefore, will result in a financial deficit for the SOE. One of the factors that could conceivably lead to overestimation of capacity utilization is the inclusion of inefficient plants in the measurement. Such a pitfall can be avoided by simply shutting down the inefficient plants. The resulting contraction in output will necessarily cause the cost

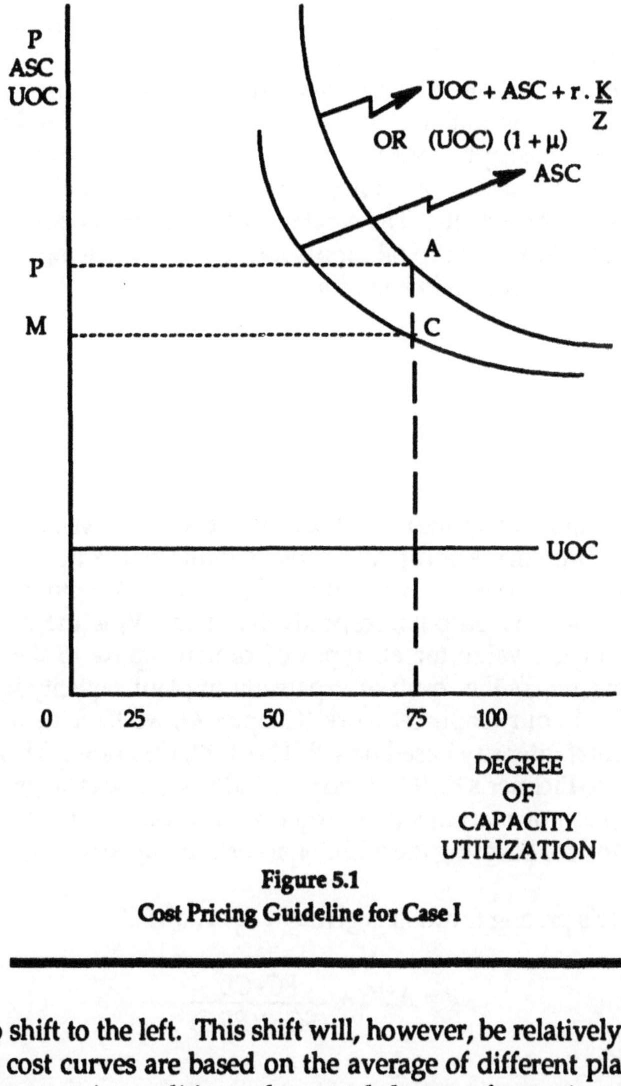

Figure 5.1
Cost Pricing Guideline for Case I

curve to shift to the left. This shift will, however, be relatively small since indirect cost curves are based on the average of different plants. Under normal economic conditions, the actual degree of capacity utilization is usually less than the installed capacity. This unutilized capacity serves as a reserve for unforeseen circumstances. Since the ASC+UOC curve lies below the true cost (UOC+ASC+r[K/Z]) curve, it is obvious that SOEs could generate a surplus at all levels of capacity utilization (See, for example, the area MPAC in Figure 5.1).

Eichner (1983, 146-147) bases his justification of the use of markup pricing on two considerations: the secular rate of growth of industry, "g_j", and the incremental capital-output ratio, "V_j". The former factor is dependent upon the increase in output per worker, price elasticity, and the industry's income elasticity. The capital-output ratio depends on the cost of purchasing additional capital inputs needed for increasing capacity by a given amount, as shown in equation 5.6.

$$V_j = \sum_{i=1}^{n} \frac{P_i k_{ij}}{P_j Q_j} \qquad (5.6)$$

In this equation, k_{ij} indicates the elements of the K vector that show the necessary purchases of capital goods by industry j from industry i for the expansion of output by a magnitude of Q_j. P_i and P_j stand for the price of capital inputs and outputs, respectively. Thus, V_j is the ratio of the summation of the value for all types of capital inputs to the value of produced output, as the result of expansion in plant capacity by a magnitude of Q_j. In our empirical work (Chapter 4), we have developed an index of capital intensity based on (IP/IT)+ (OP/OT) ratio. This index is very similar to Eichner's K_{ij}/Q_j. Since our index yields a ratio greater than V_j, the adoption of markups and target rates of return are required for expansion and for covering the additional costs arising from capital-intensity.

Eichner's pricing formula is given in equation 5.7.

$$P = AVC + \frac{FC+CL}{(SOR)(ERC)} \qquad (5.7)$$

or

$$P = AVC + AFC + ACL$$

AVC = Average variable cost,
AFC = Average fixed cost,
ACL = Average corporate levy,
SOR = Standard operating ratio,

ERC = Engineer rated capacity,
(SOR)(ERC) = Best estimate of expected sales.

Parenthetically, we may add that Samuelson has pointed out that a factor similar to ACL is used in Soviet-type economies for funding their capital formation (Eichner 1976, 269).

Kalecki's model, somewhat different from Eichner's, is given in equations 5.8 and 5.9.

$$P = mu + n\bar{p} \tag{5.8}$$

or

$$\bar{P} = (1+\mu)\bar{u} \tag{5.9}$$

$\bar{P}$ = Weighted average price for all firms,
P = Firm's price,
u and $\bar{u}$ = Unit prime costs and weighted averages of the prime costs of the industry, respectively.

Both m and n are positive coefficients and characterize the firm's position within one industry. The weighted average of these coefficients determines the markup. Thus, the markup, μ, depends upon the degree of monopoly in that firm's position within the industry.

Although Eichner's ACL is similar to 'r(K/Z)' in equation 5.5 and Kalecki's 'μū' in equation 5.9, Eichner is critical of Kalecki's approach on the grounds that the latter has not provided an explanation of the factor that determines the magnitude of 'm'. Similarly, Lee (1984, 6-7) argues that Kalecki's pricing formula is primitive because he "combined the overhead costs and margin for profits in determining the margin to be added to costs to set the prices." Semmler (1984, 42) contends that markups are independent of the concentration ratios and, hence, finds Kalecki's model inadequate. He argues that the magnitude of markups may differ from enterprise to enterprise, depending on differences in their capital/output ratios. Such differences can exist even in a perfectly competitive model with a uniform rate of profit.

Case II

When an SOE has a mixture of commercial objectives and NCOs and is engaged in multiplant production of a single product, the government should bear the cost of NCOs. In such cases, the price that consumers pay will be different from the price received by the SOE, and, theoretically, this difference is equal to per unit cost added on by the NCOs. In this case, the price formation is illustrated by equation 5.10.

$$P^* = (1+\mu)[(1-g)(UOC^*)] \quad \textbf{(5.10)}$$

P^* = Price that the consumers are charged,
μ = Markup,
g = Percentage increase in variable cost as a result of NCOs,
UOC^* = Unit operating cost included per unit cost of NCOs.

This formulation is presented graphically in Figure 5.2. In this diagram, the horizontal axis represents the degree of capacity utilization, and the prices, costs (including the costs of NCOs), and markups are shown along the vertical axis. Here again, the ASC curve lies below the true cost curve, and the gap between the two at any level of capacity utilization represents the cost of NCOs. In the diagram, P^*P' is the per unit costs of NCOs where P^* is the price paid by consumers and P' is the price received by the enterprise. The total cost of NCOs when the rate of capacity utilization is 70 percent is given by the rectangle $MP'AC$. However, if the rate of capacity utilization relative to total demand for the product is overestimated (that is, if ex-ante is greater than ex-post), it may result in additional losses to the SOE. Point M on the vertical axis is the per unit ASC+UOC at the same level of capacity utilization. Thus, the rectangle MP^*BC shows the extent of internally generated funds through markups that are available to the SOE for expansion. If a government fails to absorb the cost of NCOs (rectangle $P^*P'AB$), to that extent it will reduce the availability of internally generated funds and, thus, prove inimical to the expansion of an SOE. The government may use any one of several alternatives to finance the cost of NCOs. Normally, governments use monies from general revenues derived from taxation. They can use public loans for the same purpose since it is known that governments have very soft budget constraints. But in the long

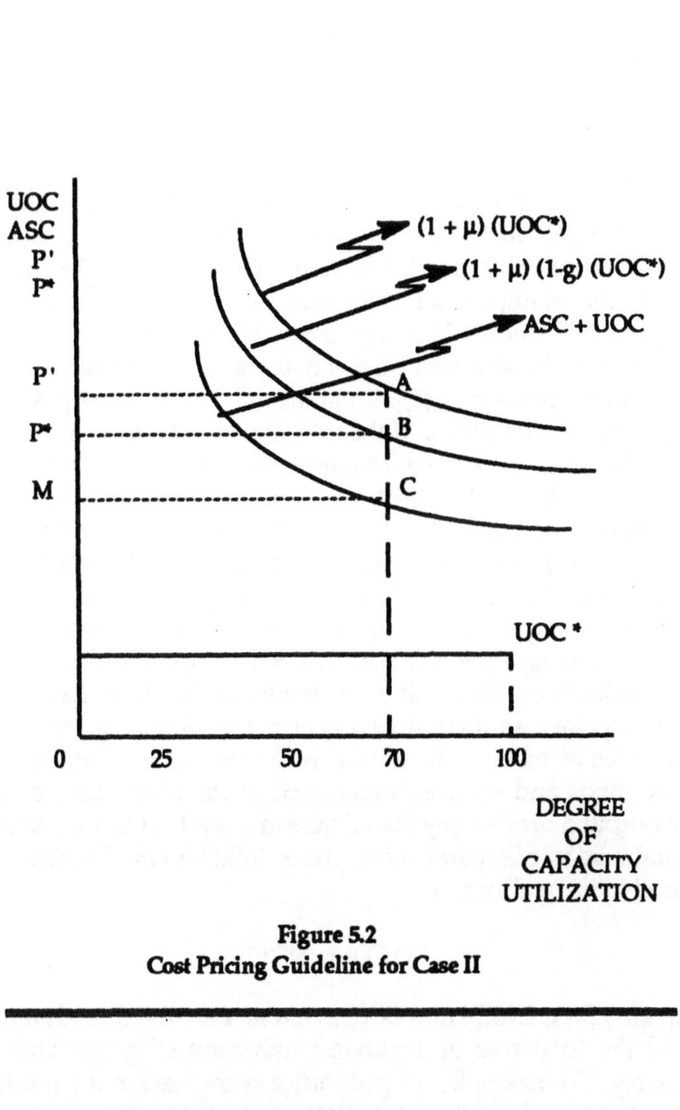

Figure 5.2
Cost Pricing Guideline for Case II

---

run, the costs of NCOs, including interest and principal, should be paid by taxpayers. For example, Walstedt (1980, 119) points out that "the cost structure of state manufacturing enterprises in Turkey is abnormally and unevenly burdened with indirect taxes."

Economies of Scale and Scope in Multiproduct SOEs

In Cases I and II, it was assumed that the SOEs were engaged in multiplant and single product operations. However, SOEs are often involved in both multiplant and multiproduct activities. Frequently, these products are joint products with joint cost characteristics. Studying the activities of an SOE in the framework of joint characteristics is more realistic as it allows for the introduction of economies of scope. For this purpose, we divide the multiproduct SOEs into two main categories--direct and indirect multiproducts. The expression "direct multiproducts" refers to those situations in which an SOE actually and simultaneously produces more than one product, e.g., simultaneous provision of passenger and freight services in railroads. If the introduction of a time element and/or quality differentiation were to change a single product to a multiproduct, then we shall call it an "indirect multiproduct," e.g., introduction of time into the production of utilities. Whether the multiproduct is direct or indirect, its cost/price structures may be analyzed with the help of the new concept of economies of scope first introduced by Willig and Panzar in 1975. Economies of scope arise from more efficient utilization of factors of production. This effective usage of factors may be in the form of either joint or share utilization. Recognition of the indivisibility of fixed assets of a public enterprise is an alternative way of stating the reason for the existence of economies of scope. These exist when the same enterprise produces different goods and services, diversified or nondiversified, at a specific level of output more cheaply than if the same level of output was produced by a combination of separate enterprises. Mathematically, this concept is expressed in inequality 5.11.

$$C(\Sigma Q_i) < \Sigma C(Q_i) \qquad (5.11)$$

In inequality 5.11, $C(\Sigma Q_i)$ and $\Sigma C(Q_i)$ denote the total cost of joint production and the total cost of separate production of goods and services, respectively. For example, if a post office is engaged in the production of three kinds of services--first class (Q1), second class (Q2), and third class (Q3) mail--economies of scope may be illustrated by inequality 5.12.

$$C(Q1,Q2,Q3) < C(Q1,0,0) + C(0,Q2,0) + C(0,0,Q3) \qquad (5.12)$$

The degree of economies of scope (DES) is given "by the proportion of the cost of joint production that is saved by joint production." Thus,

$$DES = \frac{\Sigma C(Q_i) - C(\Sigma Q_i)}{C(\Sigma Q_i)} \qquad (5.13)$$

Again, we may use the post office example to illustrate the use of 5.13, as follows:

$$DES = \frac{C(Q1,0,0) + C(0,Q2,0) + C(0,0,Q3) - C(Q1,Q2,Q3)}{C(Q1,Q2,Q3)} \quad (5.14)$$

Economies of scope exist when this ratio is more than 0, and diseconomies when it is less than 0.

Since the SOEs are engaged in the production of joint and multi-products either directly or indirectly, it is important to incorporate economies of scale and economies of scope to properly analyze the cost and price structures. If the impact of these two concepts on the behavior of costs is ignored, we are left with the old, neoclassical cost function that is both biased and abstract from reality. A 1982 study by Baumol, Panzar, and Willig showed that whenever an enterprise is engaged in multiproduct activities the conventional measures of average cost may be inaccurate. Semmler in 1984 demonstrated that such measures were far from perfect and in some cases simply could not even be defined. The inaccuracy of average cost in conventional analysis results from the unrealistic aggregation of heterogeneous outputs in a multiproduct enterprise. Moreover, a change in the composition of outputs also changes the costs of production. We must take into account the effect of changes in the composition of output on cost, economies of scope, transversity, and convexity used by Baumol, Panzar, and Willig (1982). To overcome the inaccuracy of conventional methods, they have suggested the use of Average Incremental Cost (AIC), which reflects reality and the specific characteristics of multiproduct activities more accurately. They define AIC as changes in total costs that may be attributed to specific levels of output. First, they are compared to zero production, then divided by the actual production level of output. For instance, in the post office example, AIC for second class mail, AIC(Q2), may be found as follows:

$$AIC(Q2) = \frac{C(Q1,Q2,Q3) - C(0,Q2,0)}{Q2} \quad (5.15)$$

C(Q1,Q2,Q3) = Total cost for the three multiproducts together,
C(0,Q2,0) = Cost attributed to second class mail,
Q2 = Volume of second class mail.

Some limited empirical work has been done on multiproduct cost functions. A few of these studies have been collected by Bailey and Friedlaender (1982). They may indicate the usefulness of the concepts of economies of scope and scale in analyzing the costs of SOEs. Among these studies, we find estimates of multiproduct cost functions for hospitals (Cowing and Holtman 1981), economies of scale and scope in the telecommunications industry (Fuss and Waverman 1981), and multiproduct analysis of railroads (Jara-Diaz and Winston 1981). Bailey and Friedlaender use these studies to show the necessity for disaggregating output and then conclude that ignoring the multiproduct nature of an enterprise may result in a seriously biased estimation of the cost. The concept of economies of scope seems to provide a useful tool that could throw some light on the dark areas of efficiency, pricing procedures, and other behavioral characteristics of SOEs. There are, however, some unanswered questions. For example, what is the use of this concept if disaggregation of output is not possible or simply unfeasible, or if the costs of this disaggregation, where it is possible, are too high? In conclusion, economies of scope may be used both as a complement and as a substitute for economies of scale. Where products can be disaggregated, they provide a useful and appropriate analytical tool. Bailey and Friedlaender (1982, 1028) point out that wherever economies of scope or subaddivity exists "the global cost surface cannot be represented by the traditional concepts designed to indicate the structure of costs in a single product setting." Therefore, when economies of scope and economies of scale are introduced into the analysis of the structures of SOEs, further research beyond the neoclassical theory of the production function becomes necessary.

The Classical Framework

The empirical evidence indicates that the target rates of return differ from enterprise to enterprise due to: differences in the composition, indivisibility, and mobility of capital; market structures; efficiency; NCOs; and the size of the enterprise. Although the existence of such differences does not militate against the norms of classical theory, they are completely unacceptable to neoclassicists because they violate the basic conditions of Pareto optimality and should, consequently, result in an inefficient allocation of resources. The inadequacies of the neoclassical approach to cope with the problems of economies of scope and scale lead us to explore the applicability of the classical framework to the analysis of cost/price behavior of SOEs. However, whatever theory or policy is applied, it will invariably generate controversy. Nevertheless, as Lee (1984, 2) has forcefully pointed out, any given policy must be derivable from some generally accepted theory, and we believe that the classical theory does provide a realistic framework for devising appropriate pricing policies for SOEs.

In the preceding pages, we have introduced three different approaches to oligopolistic pricing, namely, full costs, markups, and target rates of return. Lee (1984, 9) considers the three separate guidelines as different forms of the same pricing policy, and ascribes the apparent difference among these simply to different cost accounting procedures. Floyd, Gray, and Short (1984, 17) argue that "the most common method for determining prices in practice is some form of average accounting cost plus some mark-up for a profit margin." This view fits very well into the classical framework. Furthermore, the application of target rates of return fits into the classical theory, and this harmony between the two is fully supported by empirical evidence (See, for example, Pasinetti [1977], Roncaglia [1980], Harcourt [1982], Kotz [1982], Clifton [1983], Earl [1983], Schefold [1983], Eichner [1983], and Semmler [1982]--[Lee 1984, 1]).

The position taken above is not without opponents. These skeptics point out that the target rates of return are based on some kind of standard volume of output that may not necessarily be an equilibrium level of output. Thus, they contend that there may be shortages or surpluses from period to period, i.e., the average volume of output (upon which target rates of return are based) may not be a market clearing volume; hence, the preset target rates (prices) may actually be disequilibrium prices (See, for example, Thurow [1983], Tool [1979], and Okun [1981]). Lee (1984, 25) responds to the critics as follows: "There have been a number of statements made recently which have argued that full cost prices do not clear the market and hence are disequilibrium prices. Their arguments have meaning only within a neoclassical content and therefore are specific to the neoclassical version of full cost prices." Semmler (1984, 10) goes one step further and declares that, for purposes of classical fit, "prices do not necessarily have to be equilibrium prices."

The foregoing arguments relate primarily to the suitability of classical model to cost/price analysis of large, oligopolistic, private enterprises. There are, however, many similarities in the behavior of large private corporations and most SOEs. Both use large amounts of fixed capital, i.e., they are both capital-intensive. Both use some kind of markups for establishing the target rates to finance current operations and generate sufficient funds for reproduction and for expansion of capital, and both exercise financial and operational control (efficiency) over their establishments (See, for example, Bates and Fraser [1974, 82-86] and Eichner [1976, 56]). This position is supported by many economists. Semmler (1984, 183) uses the following quotation from Brown to support this thesis:

> It becomes apparent, therefore, that the analysis of price in accordance with the method outlined is closely interwoven with the method of financial control, since the expression of price policy, in terms of rate of return attainable on capital employed, is the most significant factor bearing upon the question of availability of capital for the purpose of operations.

Bates and Fraser (1974, 82) carry this argument further and uncover the same goals for SOEs. They contend that the SOEs "have taken their financial objectives first and foremost for pricing criteria." Although there are a number of similarities between large private corporations and most SOEs, there are, indeed, some very fundamental differences, too. For one thing, the target rate of return in private corporations is internally determined, but in the case of SOEs, it is of exogenous origin, having been determined by the government. In addition, private corporations do not have any NCOs, but SOEs are, more often than not, riddled with such objectives. Important as these differences are, they can be simply explained away by noting that, regardless of origins, SOEs and private corporations both have the same ultimate objective.

We feel quite comfortable in suggesting that, by and large, we can apply the same models for studying the cost/price behavior of SOEs as those that have been developed for large private corporations by Semmler in 1984. To the extent that SOEs carry the additional burden of NCOs, these models need to be modified. Furthermore, Semmler (1984, 166) confirms that:

> Modern corporate pricing does not contradict the classical notion of natural prices or the Marxian notion of production as a center of gravity for market prices, rather, it fits very well into the framework.

Before we introduce our own model, we will give a brief description of Semmler's model and the logic upon which it is based. Large corporations crystallize their needs for capital into an endogenous factor that is embodied in their markups. Semmler has derived this factor for three specific cases; Case A applies to nondifferentiated profits, Case B to differentiated profit rates for single products, and Case C to differentiated and nondifferentiated profit rates for joint products. The determination of profit rates and markups for each of these cases is illustrated by the following equations:

Case A:

$$P\bar{A}\ \langle M\rangle = PB' + rPB^{+} \tag{5.16}$$

from which the markups

$$\langle M\rangle = \langle C\rangle^{-1}\ \langle \Pi\rangle \tag{5.17}$$

Case B:

$$\bar{P}\bar{A}\ \langle M\rangle = \bar{P}B' + \bar{P}B^{+}\langle\bar{r}\rangle \tag{5.18}$$

from which the markups

$$\langle M\rangle = \langle C\rangle^{-1}\ \langle \Pi\rangle \tag{5.19}$$

Case C:

$$\bar{P}\bar{A} + \bar{P}B' + \bar{P}B^{+}\ \langle r\rangle = \bar{P}B \tag{5.20}$$

$$\bar{P}\{B - (\bar{A} + B' + B^{+}\ \langle\bar{r}\rangle)\} = 0 \tag{5.21}$$

$$\langle M\rangle = \langle C\rangle^{-1}\ \langle \Pi\rangle \tag{5.22}$$

$\bar{P}$ and P = Markup pricing vectors for differential and nondifferential profit rates, respectively, for both multiproduct and multiplant enterprises,
$\bar{A}$ = Matrix of inputs and is equal to A+dl,
A and dl = Input matrix and the matrix of consumption goods for the reproduction of labor power, respectively,
M = Diagonal matrix of different markups for products or product groups,
B' and B^{+} = Depreciation matrix and the matrix for total capital advanced per unit of output, respectively,
r and $\langle\bar{r}\rangle$ = Uniform profit rate and the matrix for the differential profit rate, respectively,

$\langle C \rangle$ in Case A = Diagonal matrix of the products of $P\bar{A}$, which are represented by the vector of production costs for A,
$\langle C \rangle$ in Case B = Diagonal matrix and the product of $P\bar{A}$, which represents the vector of production costs in B,
$\langle \Pi \rangle$ in Case A = Gross profit vector, which is a product of $PB' + rPB^{+}$,
$\langle \Pi \rangle$ in Case B = Gross profit vector, which is the product of $\bar{P}B' + \bar{P}B^{+} \langle \bar{r} \rangle$.

Semmler's model is described by expression 5.23.

$$\bar{A}X \leq BX \tag{5.23}$$

$\bar{A}$ = Square matrix of material (A) and consumption goods for reproduction of labor power (dl). The elements of matrix A represent the input i per unit of output j (i.e., $\bar{a}_{ij}$),
$\bar{A}X$ = Total input requirement,
B = Matrix of output coefficients. Each element in this matrix shows the ith output per unit of commodity j (b_{ij}),
BX = Total output.

Our adaptation of Semmler's model is based on several assumptions: that the outputs of SOEs are marketable and marketed; that the true costs of production are financed internally either by markup on prime costs or by a target rate of return on the advanced capital (circulating and fixed capital); that the SOEs are operating in oligopolistic markets; and that the SOEs may have purely commercial objectives or may have a blend of commercial objectives and NCOs. In the model below, we simply make an allowance for the cost of NCOs; the actual procedure for measuring this cost will be discussed in Chapter 6. Our model begins with the inequality given in 5.24, representing the total inputs needed for commercial objectives only and the total output produced by SOEs and the right-hand side is exclusive of noncommercial costs:

$$\{(\bar{A} - \bar{A}^{*}) + (B' - B'^{*})\}X \leq BX \tag{5.24}$$

$\bar{A}$ = Sociotechnological matrix of SOEs, which includes their utilized inputs for NCOs,
B = Depreciation matrix for fixed capital, which includes the wearing out of fixed capital as the result of SOEs meeting their

social obligations,
$\bar{A}^*$ = Portion of a sociotechnological matrix, which is related solely to noncommercial goals,
B'^* = Depreciation matrix for noncommercial goals.

Since our pricing model considers only "true" costs of production, the utilized inputs for social objectives should be deducted from $\bar{A}$ matrix. According to the contract plan, SOEs must be compensated for the costs of meeting their social objectives. This plan is explained in detail in Chapter 6.

If we assume that our price formation is based on cost of inputs necessary for commercial objectives only with some kind of oligopolistic pricing, inequality 5.24 may be written as:

$$\{B - (\bar{A} - \bar{A}^*) - (B' - B'^*)\}X \geq 0 \qquad (5.25)$$

This inequality indicates a surplus may be generated over the commercial costs of production. Both 5.24 and 5.25 are necessary conditions for growth and expansion of SOEs. If $(\bar{A} - \bar{A}^*)$ and $(B' - B'^*)$ in 5.25 are represented by L and M, respectively, then:

$$P\{L + M\}X = \langle S \rangle = \langle T \rangle \qquad (5.26)$$

where vectors P, S, and T denote prices, subsidies, and taxes. This equation indicates that the government compensates SOEs by means of taxation. Since our pricing model is based on the true costs of production, the given prices in Semmler's Case C should be adjusted by excluding the costs of noncommercial objectives.

In the following formulas, B^+ and B^{+*} denote the matrix of total capital advanced and necessary capital for the provision of NCOs.

$$P(\bar{A} - \bar{A}^*) + P(B' - B'^*) + rP(B^+ - B^{+*}) = PB \qquad (5.27)$$

or

$$rP(B^+ - B^{+*}) = P\{B - (\bar{A} - \bar{A}^*) - (B' - B'^*)\} \qquad (5.28)$$

The pricing relationships in 5.28 could be weighted by a standard volume of output and substituting $1/\lambda$ for r, i.e., its eigenvalue.

$$rP(B^+ - B^{+*})X = P\{B - (\bar{A} - \bar{A}^*) - (B' - B'^*)\}X$$

$$P(B^+ - B^{+*})X = \lambda P\{B - (\bar{A} - \bar{A}^*) - (B' - B'^*)\}X$$

In Semmler's model (1984, 166), the markup or cost-plus pricing for corporations with joint products is demonstrated in the following fashion:

$$P\bar{A}\langle\delta\rangle = PB \tag{5.29}$$

In expression 5.29, the diagonal matrix $\langle\delta\rangle$ is equal to $I + \mu$, and $\langle\mu\rangle$ is the diagonal matrix of markup. Prime cost is considered only for markup prices. When applying the above formula in our pricing model, it is necessary that A^* be subtracted from A. In the following expression, PB is exclusive of noncommercial costs:

$$P\{\bar{A} - \bar{A}^*\}\delta = PB$$

or

$$P\{\bar{A} - \bar{A}^*\}\{I + \mu\} = PB \tag{5.30}$$

Equations 5.27 and 5.30 are equal.

$$P\{\bar{A} - \bar{A}^*\} + P\{\bar{A} - \bar{A}^*\}\mu = P(\bar{A} - \bar{A}^*) + P(B' - B'^*) + rP(B^+ - B^{+*})$$

or

$$P\{\bar{A} - \bar{A}^*\}\mu = P(B' - B'^*) + rP(B^+ - B^{+*}) \tag{5.31}$$

If we assume $P\{\bar{A} - \bar{A}^*\} = G$ and the right-hand side of the above equation is equal to H, then equation 5.31 could be written in the form of equation 5.32:

$$G\langle\mu\rangle = H \tag{5.32}$$

$$\mu = G^{-1}H$$

In equation 5.32, G and H represent the vectors of necessary prime costs and gross surplus. In this model, markups are determined by $\bar{A}$, $\bar{A}^*$, B', B'^*, B^+, and B^{+*}, assuming that their profit rates and prices are given. Some redistributional goals could be achieved by this pricing procedure, because the cost of noncommercial goals is financed by taxation.

Conclusion

SOEs are, either directly or indirectly, engaged in multiproduct and joint product activities. Empirical evidence suggests that in most countries there is a target rate of return that may differ from enterprise to enterprise. We have found evidence to support the opinion that there is no conflict between the practice of markups and classical theory. In fact, this research and analysis lead to the conclusion that the classical approach is more realistic than the neoclassical doctrine of MCP. The interdependency of such interrelated factors as pricing, financing, subsidization, distributional goals, and investments fits nicely into the classical framework. Empirical evidence suggests that if, in pricing decisions, this interdependency is ignored, it can lead to serious financial problems and contraction of economic activity and in some cases to actual disinvestment. In our study, we have noted that the behavior and operational characteristics of SOEs are very similar to those of the large private corporations. Consequently, we have adapted private corporation models, with suitable modification, for the analysis of cost-price behavior of SOEs, taking into consideration the fact that there is no simple dichotomy between the former and latter enterprises with respect to their behavior and expectation for them.

6

Conflict in Micro and Macro Objectives of SOEs

In this chapter, we shall concentrate on the contradiction between the micro- and macroeconomic objectives of SOEs. The reasons why it may be impossible to employ the performance indicators used by private enterprises will also be analyzed. Alternative ways of evaluating the performance of SOEs will be investigated, and the reasons for using such alternative methods will be discussed.

Many of the SOEs in various countries purport to achieve goals that are complex, confusing, contradictory, vague, implicit, and unquantifiable. They are often mutually inconsistent and sometimes mutually exclusive. This inconsistency in goals, coupled with their vague specifications, is among the factors that might not only cause problems in evaluating the performance of SOEs but also contribute to failure in governmental control. Whenever objectives are stated in generalized form rather than in precise and specific terms, the evaluation of performance may easily deviate from objectivity, and there may be a tendency to become more subjective. In contrast to SOEs, the goals of private enterprises are precise and easily identifiable. Duality in objectives is one of the main characteristics of most SOEs. These enterprises are supposed to both function in the public interest and achieve an efficient allocation of resources. In struggling to achieve these objectives, the managers often have to make tradeoffs, especially when one goal can be achieved only at the expense of others. White (1976, 575-589) argues that these enterprises often tradeoff profits against "net pecuniary benefits." Gillis (1982, 1) states that "given the numerous 'social' goals and 'equity' responsibilities that state enterprises are typically expected to fulfill, it might be argued that, in practice, 'efficiency' is given secondary emphasis."

The question of tradeoffs between economic and noneconomic objectives also has been argued by Jones (1975, 146), Rees (1976, 23), Keyser, Windle, and Stares (1978, 165-166), Heald (1980, 263), Kim (1981, 479-482), Raiffa (1981, 55-62), Fung (1982), Gray (1983, 37), Floyd (1983, 7), Trivedi (1985, 21-23), and others. All of them seem to agree with Gillis's position. This author concurs. However, the issue of whether SOEs should be used as a tool for achieving social objectives remains to be analyzed. The use of SOEs as a means of public policy implementation could have undesirable consequences for SOEs. The cost of meeting social objectives is usually financed from different sources that may have varying macro effects on the rest of the economy. For instance, taxes could be imposed on private enterprises or households for financing SOEs. The net effect of such tax imposition depends upon the contribution of SOEs to the well-being of the society. Many economists have tried to apply a general equilibrium model internalizing all external costs and benefits to ascertain whether society is better or worse off. Their general equilibrium model was based upon such assumptions as optimization, preference ordering, etc. (Kornai 1971, 353). However, these assumptions cannot be made for activities of SOEs because the state cannot base its activities on a social welfare function that is only "an imaginative piece of fiction, never identified in reality because it is never identifiable" (Nove 1973, 65).

In some countries, SOEs have been created for political rather than economic objectives. They are involved in risky ventures for which private enterprises have neither the capacity nor the appetite. Their involvement in highly capital-intensive industries often is compounded by direct or indirect political pressures to provide NCOs. These social objectives imposed by political pressure often create conditions that conflict with the SOEs' commercial objectives. The Fabian socialists, such as Bevan, believed (as did Marx) that nationalization of industries would lead to a revolution in industrial democracy and take control of the commanding heights of the economy by the state (Redwood 1980, 7). Crosland argues that the main policy objective was a shift in the control of capital accumulation from the private to the state sector, not the efficient allocation of resources (Crosland, quoted by Nelson 1976, 63). In France, the objective of nationalization was to create a tool for resisting undue pressure from certain firms and to stimulate the economy (Dreyfus 1980, 200).

Efficiency Conditions

Samuels and Mercuro (1976, 60) interpreted economic efficiency in the following fashion:

> What economists mean by efficiency (Pareto Optimality) is complex and subject to abuse, but in general it means that in attempts to maximize results, no further gains should be sought than those which do not incur (uncompensated) losses, or that marginal benefits must be adjusted to marginal costs so that prices should reflect the social marginal valuation of resources

> in alternative uses. Efficient solutions, for example, in pricing systems, are those which satisfy or achieve this criterion; they are efficient in that they do not impose uncompensated losses and enable the realization of maximum net gains, that is, prices cover, or just cover, costs.

Neoclassical economists define efficiency in terms of pecuniary costs and benefits. In contrast, political economists evaluating SOEs consider the linkages among economic, political, and social forces. If the interaction among these forces were omitted, the outcome would be an incomplete theoretical exercise in abstraction. Because neoclassical theory ignores this interaction, it is an incomplete theory. SOEs should be studied in a sociopolitical and socioeconomic situation. To this author, it appears that the whole discussion of efficiency in the operation of SOEs seems somewhat irrelevent because the combination of commercial objectives and NCOs of SOEs makes the satisfaction of efficiency conditions difficult.

Gillis (1977 and 1982) follows the Lange-Lerner tradition for allocative efficiency. He suggests that the basis of prices for inputs and outputs should be marginal social opportunity costs. If SOEs were obligated to achieve NCOs, then the cost of these objectives, after explicit quantification, should be paid in the form of subsidies to the SOEs. Gillis also recommends that public capital receive a rate of return at least equal to the opportunity costs of capital and that all type of enterprises should be treated similarly in regard to taxation. Based on the above norms and other material presented in preceding chapters, we can conclude that these suggestions have not been applied in most cases. Thus, some misallocation of resources has prevailed in SOEs. They hire more labor than is strictly necessary because they have been used as receptacles for surplus labor. They utilize investment with a return that does not correspond to the opportunity cost of capital, arguing that investment in some areas is necessary and inevitable. Since SOEs are obligated to perform in such a manner that the public interest is guaranteed, it must be understood that there will always be some conflict between economic and social objectives. Noreng (1981, 142) argues that "public corporations permit themselves greater risks and higher rates of growth than do private corporations, paying less attention to the most efficient use of resources and capital in deference to other goals."

In this study, we have not been concerned with the investigation of the logic behind assigning social obligations to SOEs. The primary emphasis has been to show that SOEs are obligated to fulfill inconsistent, interdependent, and sometimes conflicting multiple objectives. Our intention is neither to accept the inefficient allocation of resources nor to prove that SOEs are more cost-efficient in attaining objectives. Our purpose is to analyze the arguments of those economists who have alleged that SOEs are inefficient. These economists usually compare the financial accounts of SOEs with private enterprises, but such a comparison is unrealistic. Private enterprises focus on profit as a measure of "fitness" and "rightness" for their operations; in contrast, profit has rarely been used as a measure of efficiency in SOEs because the benefits of NCOs are not reflected in the financial accounts of these enterprises. Furthermore, the primary objective of SOEs is not pecuniary gain.

Leibenstein (1978), Gillis (1977), and Brown and Jackson (1978) have classified efficiency into two categories: allocative efficiency (i.e., economic or Pareto efficiency) and technical efficiency or X-efficiency. Leibenstein (1978, 17) defines X-efficiency as follows:

> When an input is not used effectively, the difference between the actual output and maximum output attributable to that input is a measure of X-inefficiency. In this context X-efficiency is to be contrasted with allocative efficiency, the latter being the form of efficiency commonly considered in neoclassical economics.

The reasons for both kinds of inefficiency (i.e., allocative and X-inefficiency) in the case of SOEs can be attributed primarily to external factors, such as political abuse or lack of clearly defined social objectives. However, technical efficiency and allocative efficiency are interrelated and interwoven. Leibenstein (1978, 159) argues that "allocative efficiency depends on X-efficiency, and not the other way around." Stigler (1976, 213), on the other hand, is not in favor of dividing efficiency into two types because he believes that "the whole notion of X-efficiency can usefully be assimilated into the traditional theory of allocative efficiency, and can be handled within the framework of modern economic analysis."

In the introduction to this chapter, some of the characteristics and objectives of SOEs were listed. As long as these objectives are not explicit, consistent, and clearly defined, a precise measurement of performance is impossible. Furthermore, this measurement becomes complicated whenever the goals of an enterprise deviate from the original target. For instance, an industry created to support a branch of high technology later on might be forced to maintain more workers than is necessary when technology displaces workers. Since the goals of SOEs are often revised because of changes in government policies, a quantitative static measure of performance is not applicable to the dynamic conditions surrounding SOEs.

Contract Between Government and SOEs

Since the goals of SOEs usually involve commercial objectives and NCOs, there is a written or tacit agreement between the state and the SOEs that, to the extent that the cost of NCOs is identifiable, the SOEs should be reimbursed. After compensation has been made for the costs of its social objectives, the enterprise is then expected to be financially viable. However, financial viability does not guarantee that an SOE is operating efficiently because the complexity of social functions may prevent the accurate identification and measurement of its costs and benefits. Furthermore, the multiplier effects of gains in social objectives may understate the real contribution of an SOE. It may be pointed out that, in some cases, the costs of social objectives can be identified with some degree of accuracy. For example, if, in order to prevent further congestion in densely populated cities, a government commissioned an SOE to provide transportation and other services to people to encourage settlement in outlying areas, the government and the SOE could identify the cost of such social functions.

In France, the Nora Report criticized state enterprises for incurring losses that were not justified by their social functions (Sheahan 1976a, 156). The report pointed out that if the SOEs are compensated for more than the costs of their social objectives resources would be wasted in a blind, undirected transfer of income. But SOEs throughout the world have claimed that their inefficiency and the incomparability of their operations with those of the private sector are the result of their obligation to achieve social objectives. Therefore, if SOEs are compensated for the actual costs of these NCOs, their financial performance may be used as a measure of managerial efficiency. It has been alleged by some economists that in Ghana, Turkey, and Tanzania, the poor financial results of SOEs were due to corruption, special privileges, and political favors (Sheahan 1976b, 228). But poor financial performance does not necessarily indicate the existence of corruption if the tradeoffs between efficiency and the desired social objectives have not been accurately evaluated.

Micro and Macro Objectives of SOEs

In contrast to the micro objectives of private enterprises, where effort is directed toward technical efficiency and profit maximization, SOEs are designed to address problems of macro dimensions involving infrastructure facilities, establishment of heavy and basic industry, correction of imbalances in regional growth, creation of jobs, etc. By their very nature, therefore, the SOEs require heavy outlays. In Argentina in 1965, when the government imposed price controls, the state railway accounted for 20 percent of the central government's total deficit. A significant portion of the government deficit in Argentina at that time consisted of subsidies to other public enterprises that were not making profits (Chu and Feltenstein 1978, 454).

Throughout the world, SOEs have been criticized because they are not financially viable and their deficits are often a burden on their governments. We would like to point out that financial viability is seldom the primary objective when an SOE is established. Other objectives--the provision of jobs, anti-inflation policies, or other social goals--are really the primary concerns. In support of this argument, the empirical study done by Kim (1981, 471-484) may be cited. He compared the performance of twenty-three private and twelve public manufacturing enterprises in Tanzania. All the public enterprises claimed they were meeting commercial objectives. Kim, however, found that the SOEs had sizable losses, but private enterprises were often profitable. He also found that the SOEs had lower productivity because they were obligated to hire more labor than was necessary. Labor's share in gross product, a ratio of the wage rate per man-hour to the value added per man-hour for private and state enterprises, was .38 and .58 thousand shillings (Tsh), respectively. Also, the value added per man-hour was 9.73 Tsh and 8.13 Tsh for private and state enterprises, respectively. The output per unit of capital was also lower in the SOEs. Kim concluded that the SOEs were forced to meet social goals even though they were established for commercial objectives. It follows that, despite disclaimers, an SOE usually has dual objectives. Therefore, it is very difficult to accurately assess the performance of an SOE in terms of its officially stated objectives.

In most countries, in setting up SOEs, questions on the most efficient allocation of resources have taken second place to questions of industrialization, modernization, and regional development through investment in underdeveloping regions. In different countries, SOEs have been used either as direct instruments or as pipelines for solving the problems of regional development in a series of particular and fragmented programs. The establishment of steel plants in southern Italy and shipyards in northern Sweden are examples of the use of SOEs as engines of growth in economically and technologically underdeveloping areas.

Commenting on the astonishing success of the Italian experiment, Allen (1972, 179) has this to say:

> IRI's contribution to regional development in the South has been so large that it raises the question whether other countries with serious regional problems would be advised to create a similar institution with a similar obligation to assist the economies of their less prosperous areas.

These measures undoubtedly have brought about quantitative and qualitative improvements in depressed areas, as a result of which the society as a whole had to bear heavy costs and which, on occasion, may have involved sacrifices. Commenting on the expectations of socioeconomic planners in Turkey, Walstedt (1980, 88) says that:

> The planners want industrialization, meaning essentially heavy industry, right now. They would like to avoid costly errors and inefficiencies, but, if these occur, the Turkish people must accept sacrifice.

The extent of these sacrifices can be gauged from the fact that economic returns from Turkish industries such as steel, pulp, petrochemicals, and fertilizers (all government owned and operated), have been far below the acceptable level. Similarly, Eltis (1979, 8) argues that, investment dollar for dollar, the output of SOEs in England has been invariably much lower than that of their private counterparts. Eltis appears to view the excessive use of capital by SOEs in relation to their output as an indication of their inefficiency, but he does not compare firms with similar characteristics.

From these examples, it would appear that the SOEs are, to some extent, a drain on society's scarce resources. But there is another side of the picture that these examples and their advocates have obviously not taken into account. Frequently, if not always, the sacrifices the society is called upon to make are accompanied by impressive compensatory social gains. Investment by SOEs has served to stimulate private investment in depressed areas, and the result of investments by both sectors has been an expansion in the number of jobs and a concomitant reduction in the rate of migration to more prosperous areas. Therefore, it follows that SOEs in a society with chronic unemployment would function more as a social welfare agent than as a purely economic agent. In such economies, privatization, closing plants, and laying off workers, although economically desirable, may be socially undesirable. Mitchell, Manning, and Acton (1978, 43) emphasize that whenever there is a conflict between micro objectives (e.g., efficiency) and macro objectives (e.g., employment creation), "this is a conflict of social priorities or values, and for this reason economic science can be of only limited help in making a policy choice."

We also believe that microeconomic intervention often becomes necessary to achieve macroeconomic goals because these objectives simply cannot be attained in a market economy that relies solely on the "Smithian invisible hand" or, for that matter, even in those economies where "Keynesian demand management" is used (Holland 1972, 6). The experience of the last few decades in England, Sweden, and Italy indicates that the "Indian summer" of both schools of thought is over. For example, Prodi (1974, 57) contends that:

> The Italian economy, in Saraceno's analysis, is unable to respond positively to Keynesian stimuli of demand; therefore it needs structural reforms which only the public sector is in a position to offer, be it through direct intervention in the economy or through an adequate planning policy.

From the study of SOEs in different countries, we have arrived at the following conclusions: First, we have used a ratio of the percentage share of the output of SOEs in GDP at factor cost, OP/OT, to the percentage share of investment in gross fixed capital formation, IP/IT, to demonstrate value of output per unit of capital. Our cross-sectional studies show that this ratio is less than 1 in both industrial and developing countries, although in the former the ratio is larger than in the latter (0.86 vs. 0.31). Table 2.2 and Appendix A2.1 show the results of our empirical studies in regard to value of output per unit of capital. The actual value will depend upon the scope of public policies adopted and the degree of divisibility possible in the given investment. Often the objective of public policy is to keep relative prices low. When SOEs are subject to government pressure, they may fail to raise prices as fast as their private counterparts. Price flexibility is limited whenever industries are highly capital-intensive because they need to cover the costs of capital and minimize fluctuations in their cash flow. Some of the enterprises are in stagnation or in a crisis stage, such as railways, steel, and shipbuilding. Thus, the specific characteristics and objectives of SOEs squeeze their revenue. In such cases, public policy has prevented SOEs from taking full advantage of their monopoly position. Our second conclusion is that the objective functions of SOEs are more complex than those of private enterprises. This complexity and the use of vague implicit goals that display variability over time make it very difficult to use a quantifiable index for measuring the performance of SOEs. Moreover, the primary objective of many SOEs is not really commercial, but the professed commercial goals are often really aimed at achieving some other public policy goals.

Measured by the norms of neoclassical theory, SOEs would be seen as entities operating in a "compounding inefficient" manner. This refers to those cases where both labor and capital are allocated in an uneconomical fashion, as a consequence of which the neoclassical marginality conditions are not satisfied. The adoption of target rates of return and markup pricing may create financial viability, but will not necessarily guarantee cost efficiency whenever the enterprise uses more factors of production than is strictly necessary. Positive, negative, or small profit does not tell anything about efficiency, unless cost minimization is also taken into account. The cost of inefficiency may be partially or totally imposed on the consumer, either directly by high prices or indirectly by taxation.

The Goal Attainment Model

In any efficiency study of SOEs, a careful separation of objectives is absolutely necessary whenever possible. By decomposition of objectives into commercial and social components, we may be able to create a series of quantitative and qualitative indicators. But the cost estimation for NCOs becomes problematic when separation of objectives is either impossible or prohibitively expensive. Some of the costs and revenue losses incurred by SOEs because of their obligation to follow government directives may be estimated by comparing SOEs with similar "baseline" enterprises that are not obligated to meet any NCOs. Such enterprises are assumed to utilize their factors of production in an efficient manner and earn a normal profit.

The costs of some social objectives, such as anti-inflation, job creation, job preservation, and regional development, may be estimated by a comparison of SOEs and private enterprises. For instance, in the case of job preservation by SOEs during a recessionary period, we might apply a "coefficient derived from modern private sector's employment response to business downturns" (Gray 1983, 55). With regard to the contribution of SOEs toward regional equity, Gray (1983, 59) suggests that:

> The appropriate baseline with which to compare the contribution of public enterprise toward regional equity is a pro-

> gram of subsidies and other incentives by which government would seek to attract private investment, domestic or foreign, into less developed regions.

In general, the estimation of cost and revenue loss resulting from the pursuit of social objectives could be made by a comparison with an alternative baseline industrial organization. These could be either private or nonprofit organizations. Cost calculation would be more accurate if the costs of a number of producers are averaged. On the basis of this comparison, the difference between standardized cost (the averaged producer cost) and the SOEs' actual cost (including the costs of their social objective) could then be used to determine the amount needed for a lump sum subsidy. Since our cost estimation is only a proxy, either because of the nature of the costs or our inability to identify all the costs of noneconomic objectives like status, power, and prestige, we should allow for some deviation from the actual cost. Therefore, we need to recognize a possible zone of bias or a reasonable confidence interval before specifying the actual amount of subsidy for a social function. If separation of objectives is not feasible, then only qualitative indicators must be used. These indicators may include the achievement of predetermined socioeconomic and sociopolitical ends and should be studied independently from economic efficiency. The sociopolitical obligations will influence the economic profitability of an enterprise by affecting its costs and revenues.

Advocates of property rights, such as Alchian (1965), argue that public ownership is inherently less efficient than private ownership, although Peltzman (1971) believes the market structure is the cause of efficiency differentials. He predicts superior efficiency in markets characterized by effective competition among firms. Both Peltzman and Alchian state an economic truism that is inapplicable in the case of SOEs because their goals are socioeconomic in nature rather than purely economic, as in private enterprises. The proper evaluation of SOEs should be based on a "goal attainment model," that is, the success or failure of an SOE must be judged on the basis of its goal attainment. Identifying goals and measuring their achievement are critical in the applicability of this model. In goal attainment strategy, we are not concerned with the mechanisms and logic behind the assigned social objectives but with whether these goals were actually attained. In other words, the variation between target goals and attained goals is our primary interest. Because of multiple objectives, ranking should be based on their assigned priorities if the need for tradeoffs among goals should arise. For instance, if the social objective for railway services is to provide transportation to rural areas, their cost may conceivably exceed the revenue generated, thus creating a tradeoff between the provision of transportation service in rural areas on the one hand and the sacrifice of revenues on the other.

"Efficiency" and "effectiveness" should not be confused or used interchangeably because the former refers to ratio of input to output, and the latter indicates the extent to which the desired objectives have been attained. This distinction between efficiency and effectiveness is important whenever the amount of subsidy is under consideration. If SOEs are obligated to attain social objectives, then subsidization should be based on the degree of success in meeting these goals. Some economists, such as Redwood and Hatch (1982, 104) and Pryke (1981, 215-219), seem confused about efficiency and effectiveness. Pryke, for example, in responding to a question on whether SOEs were efficient, recommended the use of a test such as demand satisfaction. In commercial objectives, the index of efficiency is realistic but for NCOs, the index of effectiveness is appropriate. The most effective means are not necessarily the most efficient and vice versa. Thus, there may often be a conflict between the former and the latter. For instance, the overemployment and anti-inflation policies of SOEs often conflict with their financial viability. Shifts in priorities among goals often influence efficiency and effectiveness. Thus, judgments based solely on the financial accounts of SOEs, which is a simple quantitative indicator, often give a misleading measure of their overall performance, especially if the enterprise under study is obligated to attain multiple and conflicting objectives. This inadequacy of financial accounts in measuring the overall performance for SOEs has led to a search for some suitable combination of indicators. For instance, in 1979, England's Central Transport Committee and the National Council for the post office suggested the use of both business and social indicators, e.g., multiple indicators (Redwood and Hatch 1982, 109).

The Application of Goal Attainment Model to Evaluate SOEs

France in the late 1960s and Senegal since 1980 have started to move in a more positive direction for evaluating the performance of SOEs. In these countries, there is a quasi-contractual agreement between the state and its enterprises known as the *contrats de programme* or the "contracts plan." Dreyfus (1980, 206) defined the contracts plan as "a system under which government and company management jointly lay down general objectives, specify their reciprocal obligations, and define certain indicators calling for a possible revision of contract." Based on a contract plan, the government becomes fully responsible for the costs of any NCOs it has imposed on the SOE. The magnitude of these costs is determined by negotiation between the government and the SOE prior to the adoption of the contract. This contract model, however, should be adopted with the provision for a periodic review.

Among the advantages of a contract plan is an increase in both accountability and autonomy. When such a contract between the state and enterprises exists, the managers may choose alternative strategies as they seek to achieve preset objectives. This clarification of the functions and responsibilities of SOE managers is likely to lead to a reduction in the degree of political interference. This, coupled with the freedom of management regarding strategic choices, permits the managers to operate in a more efficient manner. The autonomy of management is guaranteed by the contract as long as the managers achieve their social objectives. On the other hand, a contract plan permits a government to closely monitor the operations of an SOE.

In our pricing model discussed in Chapter 5, the costs of commercial objectives are to be financed internally by means of markup pricing and, based on the contract plan, the cost of NCOs is to be met by government subsidies. To make the contract plan more accurate as a means of performance evaluation, both explicit and implicit subsidies should be embodied in calculations of costs and subsidies. If implicit subsidies, such as inputs and cross-subsidies, are excluded from our calculations, the contract plan becomes an inaccurate tool of performance evaluation. Subsidies, costs, and revenue losses should be identified for the period specified by the agreement. This approach could be called an "ex-ante contract plan." A comparison of ex-ante and ex-post subsidies should be used as a means of performance evaluation. Two different situations could arise from this comparison.

Case I

The first possibility might be an equality between ex-ante or planned subsidies (SP) and ex-post or actual subsidies (SA). If variance between ex-ante and ex-post subsidies approached zero, this would imply that the enterprise had operated in an effective manner. The expense and revenue losses of an SOE as the result of NCOs are equal to both explicit and implicit subsidies. AC and $AC_{P'}$, respectively, denote average cost excluding costs

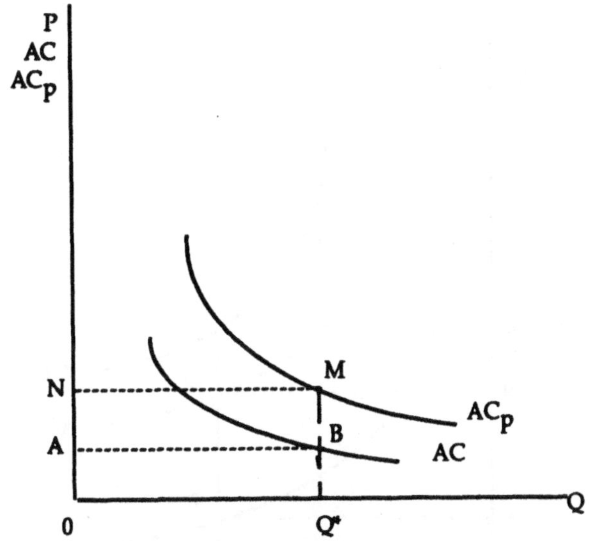

Figure 6.1
Case I, When Planned and Acutal Subsidies Are Equivalent

of social objectives and average cost including the cost of social objectives. If markup pricing is assumed, for output level (Q^*) the amount of subsidies is given by the rectangle ABMN in Figure 6.1. This rectangle is equal to the expected expenses incurred as a result of social objectives.

Case II

The second possibility is an inequality between SP and SA. However, deviation between these two should not necessarily be considered a sign of ineffective operation in an SOE since a discrepancy between two subsidies could arise as a result of external factors, or there may have been erroneous projections or measurements of either the costs of NCOs or the costs of factors of production. Some variation in costs may be expected whenever a study is within the framework of partial equilibrium analysis.

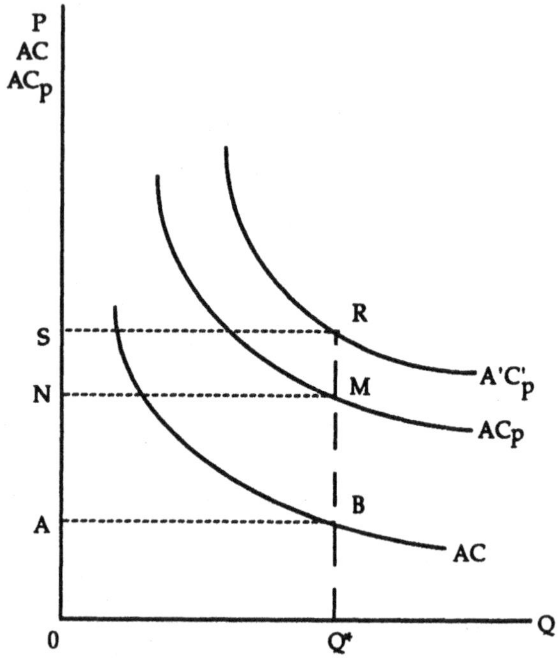

Figure 6.2
Case II, When Planned and Actual Subsidies Are Unequal

In Figure 6.2, AC_p is shifted to $A'C'_p$ as the result of the underestimation in the initial cost of NCOs. In such circumstances, the SOEs must be reimbursed for their entire deficit, which is equal to the rectangular area bounded by ABRS in Figure 6.2. The area bounded by NMRS shows the deviation between SA and SP as the result of a projection error in estimating the costs of NCOs. Thus, an "ex-ante contract plan" should be adjusted for erroneous projections before it is used as an index for managerial performance evaluation.

When there is an error in the estimation of commercial costs of an SOE, the choice of policy implementation by the government may be

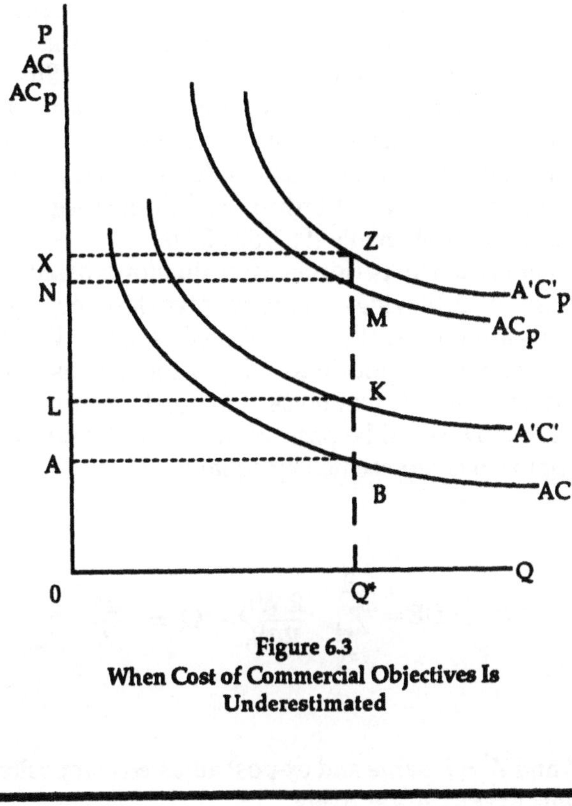

Figure 6.3
When Cost of Commercial Objectives Is Underestimated

limited in the short run, but in the long run the government will have a number of different options. It could either increase its subsidy to SOEs, let them raise prices of their products, and/or use some combination of the two. In the contract plan, the government is obligated to subsidize SOEs only for the costs of NCOs. If the costs of commercial operations were underestimated, AC and AC_p in Figure 6.3 would shift up to A′C′ and $A'C'_p$, respectively. The government subsidy to the SOE would only be equal to ABMN, and the erroneous projections of costs of commercial objectives shown by the area ABKL or NMZX should be financed by an increase in prices from OA to OL.

In conclusion, the contract plan helps to clarify and distinguish between commercial objectives and NCOs and their respective costs. This formal agreement helps both sides of the contract to cooperate in a more constructive and consistent manner, especially when the success of contracts requires substantial commitments by both parties. Since the contract is based on transparency (i.e., the separation and distinction between commercial and social objectives), the source of deficits can be identified. It may be added that this contract plan model is similar to the relative cost reduction criterion used by the British Steel Committee on nationalized industries (Greece and Mainiatis 1967, 576-589).

Another approach for performance evaluation is based on the "degree of effectiveness" in achieving ex-ante or predetermined goals. In this approach, goals are ranked (R) and assigned weights (W) in accordance with their predetermined priorities. The factor Ω is used to reflect the negative impact of contradictory goals. If the goals are in conflict with each other, the value of Ω would be positive; if no conflict exists, it will equal zero. This approach is represented by equation 6.1.

$$DE = \sum_{i=1}^{n} \frac{R_i W^*_i}{R_i W_i} - \Omega = \frac{Z^*}{Z} \tag{6.1}$$

Z and Z^* = Ex-ante and ex-post adjusted composite weight and rank (CWR), respectively,
Ω = Adjustment factor for negative impact of conflicting objectives,
$R_i W_i$ = Ex-ante weighted performance of an SOE seeking the attainment of various goals,
$R_i W^*_i$ = Ex-post target goals,
DE = Degree of effectiveness, the ratio of ex-post to ex-ante goals $i=1,\dots,n$.

If DE is greater than one, it would mean the initial expectations from the SOE were underestimated and vice versa. The closer the ratio is to one, the better the degree of effectiveness, assuming that the initial level of expectations was accurate. If a monetary value were placed on all social objectives, a rather unrealistic assumption, equation 6.1 could be written in the form of equation 6.2.

$$DE = \sum_{i=1}^{n} \frac{Z^{*}m - C^{*}}{Zm - C} \tag{6.2}$$

Zm and $Z^{*}m$ = Composite weight and rank in monetary terms for ex-ante and ex-post, respectively,
C and C^{*} = Ex-ante and ex-post costs of social objectives, subject to adjustment for unforeseen events,
i=1,...,n.

Equation 6.2 is based on a composite indicator in which positive and negative weights are given to benefits and costs, respectively. If the framework of equation 6.2 were accepted, it could be used as a measure of effectiveness.

Berczi (1978, 66) attempted to quantify in money terms the degree of effectiveness of government projects by means of an operation performance measurement index. He claimed his proposed indexes were applicable to any government program, but this is difficult to accept. Berczi's index might be inapplicable because his indexes for measuring performance are based on the assumption that we can assign monetary value to all benefits from government activities. In our procedure, it is assumed that social objectives might be ranked and weighted on the basis of social priorities. Berczi's indexes are based on a clear subdivision of the output into three consecutive levels, and each output is an input for the next step (Berczi 1978, 70). In our procedure, however, classification is based on the outcome of the highest rank. Berczi's indexes are based on the simultaneous achievement of both effective and efficient utilization of resources. In his words, "our objective must be, do the right things (i.e., efficiency) right (i.e., effectiveness)" (Berczi 1978, 66). But we do not believe that simultaneous achievement of both efficiency and effectiveness is possible in all circumstances.

Demonstrable Biases

Many economists, including Eltis (1979, 17), Savas (1980, 265), Pryke (1980, 230), Kim (1981, 475), Gillis (1982, 7), Vickers and Yarrow (1988, 143), have been critical of the performance of SOEs. Their many hostile criticisms are based primarily on a comparison of the financial accounts of SOEs with those of either all private enterprises (Eltis, 1979) or a single enterprise (Pryke, 1980 and Gillis, 1982). In the following pages, we shall summarize some of the few available studies and discuss their biases. Vickers and Yarrow (1988, 143) compared the profitability of public corporations and private companies between 1975 and 1985 (See Table 6.1). They conclude that, "on the average, the ratio of gross trading profit (before allowance for stock appreciation and depreciation) to net capital stock for privately owned companies has been about three times higher than the nearest equivalent measure for public corporations (the ratio of gross trading surplus to net capital stock)."

Eltis also criticized SOEs in the U.K. because they generate a smaller surplus than private enterprises. Table 6.2 shows the average rate of surplus for public enterprises between 1961 and 1977 was 11.1 percent, against 35.9 percent for private enterprises. He argues that financing the operations of SOEs could prove to be counterproductive and thus hinder the attainment of social objectives. He bases his argument on the empirical data used to demonstrate that the public sector often absorbs more marketed output than it actually produces. He concludes that financing the operations of SOEs is a burden on private enterprises. In contrast, Jones (1975, 11) argues that SOEs have been expanded to support and subsidize the growth of private capital. SOEs perform their "supportive role" by selling their output below their costs of production and thus provide an external benefit to the private sector. In Jones's view, the activities of the state are seen as complementary to private enterprise, not as a burden, as Eltis claimed. Other economists, such as Semmler (1982, 11-12), agree with Jones.

Still another study by Kim (1981) confirms that private manufacturing enterprise in Tanzania had better financial performances than state manufacturing enterprises during the six years 1970 through 1975. The result of this study is explained earlier in this chapter and is summarized in Table 6.3.

Pryke (1980, 215-229) also concludes that SOEs are less efficient than private enterprises. To support his claim, he compared the rates of return between similar private and state enterprises in England; the results are shown in Table 6.4. Savas (1980, 253-269) compared public and private enterprises engaged in the provision of municipal services in the United States. He argues against the use of public enterprises, claiming that they are cost inefficient. Gillis (1982, 7) compared the cost of mining in private

TABLE 6.1
Profitability of Public Corporations and of Industrial and Commercial Companies (percentages)

Year	Public Corporations A[b]	Public Corporations B[c]	Industrial and Commercial Companies[a]
1985	5.1	2.6	21.3
1984	6.3	3.4	20.6
1983	6.8	4.8	19.4
1982	6.6	4.8	16.7
1981	5.6	4.0	16.0
1980	4.7	3.4	16.1
1979	5.0	3.6	18.3
1978	5.7	4.4	17.1
1977	6.2	4.9	17.8
1976	6.2	3.1	15.6
1975	4.9	3.1	14.6
1974	4.9	2.4	17.2
1973	6.2	4.3	18.7
1972	6.2	4.6	18.5
1971	6.0	5.3	16.8
1970	6.4	5.6	16.8

Notes:
a: Gross trading profit as a percentage of net capital stock at replacement cost.
b: Gross trading surplus as a percentage of net capital stock at replacement cost.
c: Gross trading surplus, net of subsidies, as a percentage of net capital stock at replacement cost.

Source: Vickers, J. and G. Yarrow. *Privatization: An Economic Analysis*, MIT Press, Cambridge, Massachusetts, 1988, p. 143.

TABLE 6.2
The Marketed Output Surplus as a Percentage of Net Marketed Output

Year	Private Companies	Public Corporations
1961	32.1%	1.9%
1962	33.8	6.2
1963	34.5	11.7
1964	31.5	7.3
1965	34.3	8.7
1966	35.3	3.8
1967	37.3	1.9
1968	36.7	11.9
1969	36.1	23.5
1970	36.5	18.0
1971	39.4	12.7
1972	40.1	18.9
1973	32.6	16.3
1974	29.0	0.3
1975	42.0	1.8
1976	39.4	17.0
1977	39.3	30.6

Notes:
The data in these columns are derived as follows:

$$\text{Rate of Surplus} = \frac{A - (B + C + D)}{A}$$

A: Net marketed output produced and is equivalent to revenue net of capital consumption.
B and C: Marketed output consumed in wages and interest, respectively.
D: Marketed output invested.

Source: Eltis, Walter. "The True Deficits of Public Corporations," *Lloyds Bank Review,* No. 132, January 1979, p. 17.

TABLE 6.3
Operating Surplus and Factor Productivity: Manufacturing Sector, Averaged from 1970-1975 (in thousand shilling)

	Average
Operating surplus per employee:	
Private enterprise	6,019.65
Public enterprise	-6,687.60
Value added per employee:	
Private enterprise	21,880.83
Public enterprise	18,681.10
Operating surplus as a proportion of value added:	
Private enterprise	0.1315
Public enterprise	-0.4500
Gross output per unit of operating capital:	
Private enterprise	18.795
Public enterprise	8.055

Source: This table is derived from "Enterprise Performance in Public and Private Sector: Tanzanian Experience 1970-1975," by Kwan S. Kim, *The Journal of Developing Areas*, Vol. 15, No. 3, 1981, pp. 471-484.

and state enterprises in Bolivia. He argues that "for the 20-odd private Bolivian mining firms in 1973 and 1974, production costs, at 46 percent of the gross value of sales, were markedly lower than those of the state-owned firms in 1973, and slightly lower, at 52 percent in 1974." Jones (1975, 206), in a similar comparison of private enterprises and SOEs, argues that Korean public enterprises are less cost efficient than their private counterparts. Whenever comparisons like these are made, whether in general or in particular, unintended (or intended) bias seems to influence them. To avoid any bias in comparing a private enterprise with an SOE, the objective of each needs to be identified, its cost and capital intensity estimated, its wage rate structures analyzed, and finally, the related degree of risk for each type of enterprise taken into account.

TABLE 6.4
A Comparison of the Rates of Return Between Private Enterprises and SOEs in England for Similar Industries in 1976

Type	1975	1976
Road haulage		
Public	0.7	2.50
Private	5.0	9.70
Retail chain in electricity		
Public	-	0.70
Private	-	8.00
Shipping services		
Public	-	-2.50
Private[a]	-	6.35

Note:
a: This is an average of some but not all private enterprises (primarily the Irish B and I Line and European Ferries).

Source: Pryke, Richard. "Public Enterprise in Practice: The British Experience of Nationalization During the Past Decade," in *Public and Private Enterprise in a Mixed Economy;* edited by William J. Baumol, St. Martin's Press, New York, 1980, pp. 215-229.

We have already explained that SOEs have a vast variety of objectives that may conflict with each other. For instance, in the Italian constitution,it is stated that endowment grants to the Italian Institute for Industrial Reconstruction (IRI) should not only be directed to social ends, but should also be used economically. These two goals conflict with each other, unless the maximization of social ends could be interpreted as a kind of profit maximization (Holland 1972, 185). With this kind of interpretation, the financial accounts lose their viability because they do not reflect the impact of social ends. Furthermore, SOEs often pay higher wages to their employees when wage payments include social wages. The financial performance of enterprises has been adversely affected as a result of the compound effects of overemployment and overpayment. This compound effect is stronger whenever wages are a high percentage of business costs, as in the U.S. Postal Services where wages are 80 percent of costs. In the past, wages of U.S. postal workers were growing faster than those of the

TABLE 6.5
Severance Pay (in months of base salary provided)

	Years of Service			
	5	10	20	30
Public Corporations	8.3	25.0	66.4	105.4
Private Corporations	5.8	13.5	38.4	63.8

Source: Jones, Leroy P. *Public Enterprise and Economic Development: The Korean Case*, Korean Development Institute, Seoul, Korea, 1975, p. 198.

TABLE 6.6
Comparison of Increase in Labor Costs and Prices

	% Increase in Prices 1968-76	% Increase in Staff Costs Per Unit of Output 1968-76
NCB: deep-mined coal	295.5	325.8
BSC: iron and steel	227.1	241.5
British Gas	51.9	96.6
British Rail	160.3	322.0
National and Scottish Bus Groups	193.6	245.6
British Airways	78.6	78.8
Manufacturing	144.3	178.2

Source: Pryke, Richard. "Public Enterprise in Practice: The British Experience of Nationalization During the Past Decade," in *Public and Private Enterprise in a Mixed Economy*; edited by William J. Baumol, St. Martin's Press, New York, 1980, p. 223.

rest of the economy (MacAvoy, Stanbury, Yarrow, and Zeckhauser 1989, 74). SOEs, either voluntarily (as a role model) or as the result of a high degree of unionization, pay higher total wages (Dreyfus 1980, 212 and Walstedt 1980, 27). Social wages in countries like Sweden are between 34 and 45 percent of money wages (Skandinaviska 1983, 47). In Korea, "public enterprises pay more for labor than do private enterprises, but the difference is more in ancillary benefits and working conditions than in wages and salary differentials for comparable skills" (Jones 1975, 197). A study by the Korean Ministry of Labor shows that severance pay in SOEs was 65 to 100 percent higher than in private enterprises (See Table 6.5).

The use of SOEs as a tool of anti-inflation policy will invariably result in their poor financial performance. As Table 6.6 shows, the average percentage increase in labor costs per unit of output was higher than the average percentage increase in the price of output in seven SOEs in the U.K. (Pryke 1980, 223). SOEs in Bolivia and Indonesia, due to government price controls, were allowed to charge their customers only between 50 to 57 percent of their respective costs because of governmental inflation control policies (Gillis 1982, 9). In Korea, for political considerations, prices were controlled by the economic planning board. The result of this underpricing was persistent negative profits by SOEs. Managers of SOEs are confronted with many conflicting requests and pressures from different agents and individuals. The ministers of labor press for overemployment and, at the same time, expect generous wages. The ministers of finance seek financial viability, and the pricing policy board wishes to fight inflation with lower prices. By contrast, managers of private enterprises, whose primary objective is profit maximization, have much more autonomy in making their strategic decisions.

Earlier in this chapter, we attempted to demonstrate why the use of the SOEs' financial accounts is inappropriate evidence of their poor performance. The evaluation of their performance should be based on the fulfillment of all objectives, not only on financial viability. The formal agreement (i.e., contract plan) between government and SOEs establishes a clearer and more accurate criterion for evaluating the performance of SOEs. It requires the clarification of the costs of previously obscure social objectives and demonstrates the inappropriateness of financial statements as a means of performance evaluation. The World Bank (1983, 79) reports that in some countries, such as Senegal, "most of the contracts have produced measurable improvements in SOE performance." Tradeoffs between micro and macro objectives are inevitable, and make performance evaluation inaccurate if it is based solely on financial performance. Saraceno argues that:

> ...a market economy system may fail to overcome structural problems and investment opportunities, not from an insufficiency of disposable resources, but from the manner in which the decisions are taken which employ and utilize those resources. In such cases the state should intervene directly in

> order to ensure that ventures which are viable over a longer period than that acceptable to private investors, or have external effects on the rest of the national economy, are undertaken in both the micro and macro economic interest of society as a whole. (Saraceno, quoted in Holland 1972, 243)

We believe that the participation of SOEs in long-term, highly risky, capital-intensive industries may be justified on the grounds that government has the power to socialize and spread the burden of risks and costs over a very large number of taxpayers. This ability of the government (i.e., in scope and scale) may be enhanced whenever SOEs participate in diversified and financially wide-ranging, viable economic activities, such as gas, water, banking, finance, telecommunications, and electricity. The neoclassical economists viewed some type of taxation or cross-subsidization as a disruption of "optimum optimorum" conditions. Attaining macro objectives may necessitate some discrimination against pure efficiency.

Conclusion

Throughout this chapter, we have tried to explain how SOEs become obligated to meet a series of objectives that often conflict with microeconomic goals. We also agree with those economists, such as Colas (1980, 283) and Michalet (1974, 106), who find the existing economic theory in regard to the functions of the state inadequate. The functions of SOEs are more complex than simple neoclassical theory admits. Socialist theorists are more realistic and accurate in explaining the functions of SOEs.

Investments of SOEs are channeled, either by design or by accident, into areas with uncertain or low rates of profit. This is in contrast to the behavior of private enterprises, which are more interested in direct financial consequences of their activities; SOEs are interested in both direct and indirect consequences. One of the reasons for creating SOEs in mixed economies is to achieve the ends of socialism, yet retain the framework of capitalism. SOEs are engaged in some industries, such as steel and railways, that are in crisis stages but are strategically important for the national economy. Most of the sick or stagnating industries that are capital-intensive are run by the SOEs. Their crises are compounded by the use of more labor than is necessary. Overemployment may be justified by social considerations, but it is inefficient from the neoclassical point of view. Some SOEs are primarily engaged in developing and introducing new technology. This involves risks that private enterprise neither desires nor is capable of undertaking. This situation is often compounded by the use of such industries as a means of achieving other social objectives.

The establishment of SOEs in depressed areas may be useful in eliminating poverty within an economy and among its regions. The problems of disparity, inequality, excessive immigration, and slow economic growth may be tackled by establishing a series of industrial complexes in backward regions. The role of SOEs is crucial in avoiding the "stop-and-go" syndrome so often found in economic growth. Industrialization is a cumulative process and breeds further development. The activities of SOEs should be seen as a complementary and effective mechanism for stimulating the growth of private enterprise investment in many diverse industries. In depressed regions, there is usually no shortage of labor, but the lack of investment is the main constraint in those areas. The incentive for investment by SOEs in such areas is not profit but the need to eliminate economic disparity and solve the problem of what Saraceno called "structural inadequacies" (Prodi 1974, 59).

The comparison of financial accounts between private enterprises and SOEs cannot be used as a reliable measure for performance evaluation because such profitability comparisons are misleading and irrelevant. The use of such a measure results in demonstrable biases against SOEs. Financial accounts consist of cardinal numbers that fail to consider the characteristics and nature of SOEs objectives. Comparisons and tradeoffs among competing goals are often necessary. The evaluation of SOEs' performance should, therefore, be based upon a goal attainment model, rather than solely on financial viability. A formal agreement, such as the contract plan, between government and SOEs would establish a more accurate criterion for performance evaluation.

7

Summary and Conclusions

The principal objective of this book is to demonstrate the possible contradictions between the macro and micro objectives of SOEs. The former include such objectives as employment creation, strengthening of domestic and foreign competition, economic growth, and price stability; among the micro objectives are efficiency, productivity, and an operating surplus. Many SOEs in various countries are expected to achieve goals that are complex, confusing, contradictory, vague, implicit, and frequently unquantifiable. These contradictions may be the cause of most problems faced by SOEs throughout the world. An exhaustive search of literature and an intensive study of the role of the state in owning and operating SOEs from the perspective of classical, neoclassical, and socialist economies revealed that no single traditional economic theory is adequate to explain the behavioral characteristics of SOEs.

From a historical perspective, until the end of the 1970s there was a considerable increase in the number and size of SOEs in both the developing and developed nations. However, from the beginning of the 1980s, there has been a movement in the opposite direction, i.e., toward more privatization. Broadly speaking, the reasons for the growth of SOEs may be divided into two main categories, namely, economic and sociopolitical. Among the economic causes are: the need for relatively large amounts of fixed capital, often in rather risky ventures; the government's desire to control key industries and prevent the concentration of economic power in private hands; the need to conserve scarce foreign exchange and achieve economic independence through import substitution; the need to bring about long-term structural changes, to equalize regional disparities or to prevent the widening of a technological gap; a reaction to the growth of foreign domestic private industrial giants; and in general, the desire to use as a propulsive effect to stimulate overall economic activity. In some cases, governments have justified their full intervention (that is, taking over of monopolies) on the grounds that these monopolies distort resource allocation, distribution of income, product mix, volume of output, and the distribution of products. In other cases, governments have established

SOEs or taken over private establishments to use them as a source of revenue.

The specific nature of political purposes or objectives for which SOEs are created or used may vary from country to country and from time to time within the same country, depending upon their internal and external politicoeconomic circumstances and the stage of their socioeconomic development. It has been pointed out by many economists, e.g., Sheahan, that the establishment and expansion of SOEs is based on political rather than economic objectives, especially in developing countries. Experience from around the world shows that, more often than not, political objectives conflict with economic ones, and where this is the case, governments have shown partiality toward political objectives at the expense of economic objectives. The long-run consequences of such preferences have often resulted in a loss of economic efficiency and dwindling operating surpluses.

It may be noted that, given the diversity of commercial objectives and NCOs of SOEs, the use of pure economic models to define, describe, and evaluate SOEs is wholly inadequate. Therefore, we have arrived at this definition of SOEs: productive entities that produce goods and services that are not only marketable but also marketed. Thus, the exclusion principle may be applied. They are owned and controlled by the government, and their self-financing ratios are dependent upon constraints preset by the government for economic variables and NCOs. The magnitude of their subsidies, either implicit or explicit, is identifiable.

In some quarters, it is believed that the satisfaction of Pareto optimality conditions results in the most efficient allocation of resources. But since marginality conditions do not allow for NCOs and the concomitant problems caused by the lumpiness characteristics of SOEs, their use will tend to discourage investment in many worthwhile public projects. Also, Pareto optimality conditions may not always be satisfied; for example, if an investment fails to reflect social time preferences, the equality of rate of return between private and public enterprises is not a necessary condition for efficient allocation of resources. We conclude that the investment criteria for SOEs are not necessarily consistent with private investment criteria. They have dissimilar structures, objectives, and financing sources. Some economists have utilized the LLN to derive a discount rate for SOEs. They believe that the risk of investment in SOEs would be spread over a large number of taxpayers, so that the amount of risk and uncertainty per taxpayer becomes negligible. Therefore, lower discount rates may be applied to SOEs as compared with private enterprises. The true measure of net benefit from such investment is obtained only after the subtraction of the cost of risk bearing, which has been reduced by the LLN. Thus, there will be a net gain to society if investments in SOEs take place, even if the expected rate of return from these is less than the return from private investments. We believe that using "criterion packages" based on expected objectives is more accurate than using a single criterion. Since the objectives set for SOEs often include noneconomic reasons, these criterion packages for investment evaluation should be based on goal attainment models.

The financial needs of SOEs arise from a combination of their social obligations and their engagement in risky, capital-intensive activities. The many and varied sources of finance may be divided into two main categories, namely, domestic and foreign, each with several subcategories. Our empirical study shows that a 1 percent change in GFCF necessitates a 1.06 percent increase in domestic borrowing. This regression coefficient is statistically significant at the 0.0040 level. Capital intensity and foreign financing have a positive correlation and a statistically significant regression coefficient at the 0.02 level. A 1 percent increase in capital intensity would necessitate a 0.58 percent increase in foreign financing.

The internal generation of funds is one of the most important means of financing an SOE. A comparison of self-financing ratios in private and public enterprises for countries where data were available shows that on the average, in the mid-1970s, this ratio was 76 percent for private enterprises and only 48 percent for public ones. In many countries, the continued dependence of SOEs on government subsidies has led to the transfer of ownership to private hands. But in other cases, some unprofitable industries, which are either unattractive to private enterprise or are "essential" and "necessary" for some important social objectives, are still run by the state. However, the deficits of SOEs have to be paid ultimately by the taxpayers, which is by no means always politically or economically feasible. An exhaustive survey of existing studies has shown that, so far, no specific theory of finance has been developed for SOEs. This development has been hindered mainly by the dynamic nature of modern economies and the changing priorities of government objectives. Consequently, we developed a finance theory of our own that is based on a goal attainment model and cost-plus pricing.

Our cross-sectional study of forty-six countries reveals that, by and large, SOEs are engaged in capital-intensive industries. This study, however, differs from others in the following respects: we have a much larger sample; our sample included both developed and developing nations, seventeen from the former and twenty-nine from the latter; unlike other studies that covered only a few sectors, ours covers the entire spectrum of SOEs' activities; and our study not only analyzes capital intensity but includes the concomitant financing aspects that other studies ignored. To measure the capital intensity of SOEs, we used the ratio, K, of shares of GFCF to share of GDP at factor cost. We found that the average K for the seventeen developed countries is 1.55 and for the twenty-nine developing countries 2.47. Thus, the newly developing nations have a higher capital-intensity ratio. Rapid economic growth necessitates the creation of SOEs of a certain critical size and composition in order to take advantage of economies of scale and economies of scope. All of these characteristics, coupled with a large, redundant, and highly paid labor force, create financial difficulties for SOEs. In order to study the relationship between investment and financing of SOEs, we have analyzed nine different relationships. The results of these analyses, presented in Table 4.3, show that the peculiar characteristics of SOEs do contribute to the overall deficits of these enterprises, but their deficits make a relatively small contribution to the overall deficits of government and, hence, should not be considered as a sole explanation of central government deficits.

In this book, we have shown that pricing, financing, and investment are interrelated factors. In private enterprises, these decisions are made internally, but in the case of SOEs, more often than not, they are made externally because of their NCOs. Yet, at the same time, the failure of SOEs to achieve externally set targets and the accompanying financial crises have forced governments to place more emphasis on commercial objectives, and, in some cases, even to seek profits. However, the extent of commercialization of SOEs depends on the mix of economic and noneconomic objectives that they are called upon to attain. Often the objective of public policy is to keep relative prices low. Price flexibility is limited whenever industries are highly capital-intensive because they need to cover the costs of capital and minimize fluctuations in their cash flow. Thus, the specific characteristics and objectives of SOEs squeeze their revenue.

Marginal cost pricing is a cornerstone of neoclassical theory. Neoclassical economists have contended that marginal analysis is the surest way to achieve maximum efficiency/welfare, and thus, LRMC pricing could be used as a single, "general" pricing formula. The many problems associated with the measurement of marginal costs are further compounded by such factors as multiplant and multiproduct operations, the differential in off-peak and peak hours output, etc. Furthermore, MCP is unrealistic in an economy characterized by imperfect markets. This pricing policy would result in operating deficits in the case of increasing returns to scale. Such deficits, if financed through taxation, cannot be considered "distributionally neutral" and, thus, may interfere with the optimal allocation of resources. We may, therefore, conclude that MCP is an incomplete and inadequate pricing system unless the funding of deficits is also identified. If this funding were taken into consideration, MCP would not emerge as the first choice. The doctrine of MCP suffers from lack of stability and administrative difficulties and because it involves substantial costs of monitoring its practical application. For these reasons, although SOEs were often urged by government authorities to adopt MCP, available evidence indicates that, in practice, it was never implemented. Subsequently, many governments introduced an "open strategy" for which the details of the pricing structures were to be determined by SOEs in accordance with their market circumstances. The imposition of financial targets and the requirement that SOEs cover full costs, including the opportunity cost of capital, created a pricing structure similar to that of traditional economies. Therefore, in order to achieve their financial targets and the RRR, SOEs had to base their prices on average costs with specified markups.

We know that many SOEs use highly expensive inputs, and, to take advantage of economies of scale and scope, they engage in the production of joint products. In such cases, SOEs could apply, with suitable modifications, the procedures widely used by private enterprises for estimating cost shares for decomposed joint products. If decomposed output is marketed, the costs are based on the proportion of their sales value. One indirect and external procedure for estimating sales value is based on a comparison with another enterprise that produces a single product. In recent years, the governments of many countries have begun to expect the SOEs to function more and more as commercial entities. In such cases, there is a preset target rate of return that is set differently for each industry. The "cost-plus" pricing model referred to earlier is based on this target rate of return. This model rests upon two premises, namely, that prices are not based on marginal costs and that the recommended pricing model does not conflict with the pricing policies of SOEs. Pricing with a target rate of return is similar to pricing policies of modern, large corporations that are also based on cost plus a margin. The size of markup or target rate of return depends on the specific objectives or goals that are expected to be met from the preset target rate of return.

In cases where SOEs are not expected to carry out NCOs, justification for markup in pricing policies has been indicated. In any pricing model, high capital/output ratios are inseparable from a high proportion of fixed capital; therefore, markup and target rates of return are necessary for the reproduction, expansion, and control of large amounts of fixed capital. In those cases where SOEs have no NCOs and use multiplant production for a single product, their use of markup pricing is described in equation 5.5. In a case where an SOE has a mixture of commercial objectives and NCOs and is engaged in multiplant production of a single product, the cost of latter should be borne by the government, and the differential between the price paid by consumers and the price received by the SOEs should be theoretically equal to the cost of the NCOs. In this case, the price formation is illustrated by equation 5.10. If a government fails to absorb the cost of social objectives to that extent, it will reduce the availability of internally generated funds and, thus, prove inimical to the expansion and long-run survival of SOEs.

Large modern corporations and SOEs have two fundamental differences. In the former, the target rate of return is internally determined; in the latter, it is externally determined, and unlike SOEs, private corporations have no NCOs. There are, however, many similarities between the behavior of private corporations and most SOEs. Both use large amounts of fixed capital as well as some kind of target rate of return. These similarities have led us to suggest that, generally, we could apply the same methods for studying the cost/price behavior of SOEs as those that have been developed for private corporations, with appropriate modifications to take into account the burdens of externally imposed NCOs. This view fits very well into both the classical framework and the empirical evidence. On this basis, we have developed a model to analyze the cost/price behavior of SOEs that closely approximates the one developed by Semmler (1984) for large private corporations. Large corporations, according to Semmler, crystallize their capital needs into an endogenous factor that is embodied in their markups.

Our adaptation of Semmler's model is based on several assumptions, i.e., that the outputs of SOEs are marketable and are marketed, that the true costs of production are financed internally either by markup on prime costs or by a target rate of return on the total fixed and circulating capital, that the SOEs are operating in oligopolistic markets, and, finally, that the SOEs may have either purely commercial objectives or a blend of commercial and social objectives. Since our pricing model is based on the true costs of production, costs of inputs necessary for commercial objectives only, the given prices in Semmler's model, should be adjusted. In other words, the inputs utilized for meeting NCOs should be deducted from the sociotechnological matrix (input matrix and matrix of consumption goods for labor power) and compensated for separately, in accordance with the contract plan. Where SOEs are both engaged in joint products and obligated to provide some social goals, the markup or cost-plus pricing is demonstrated in equation 5.31. Some redistributional goals could be achieved by this pricing procedure, because the cost of noncommercial goals is financed by taxation.

Some economists have criticized the performance of SOEs solely on the basis of an unsatisfactory comparison of their financial accounts with those of similar private firms. In our judgment, all these studies are biased. The performance evaluation of SOEs should be based on the fulfillment of all objectives, not only on their financial viability. The formal agreement (i.e., the contract plan) between government and SOEs establishes a clearer and more accurate criterion for evaluating the performance of SOEs. Once a contract plan is agreed upon, the government assumes full responsibility for the expense and revenue losses of SOEs as the result of NCOs. Thus, the compensation of SOEs should be based on Reversing the Burden of Proof Principle or Doctrine of Improper Burdens. If the variance between ex-ante (planned) subsidies and ex-post (actual) subsidies approached zero, assuming *ceteris paribus,* this would imply that the enterprise had operated in an effective manner. The deviation between ex-ante and ex-post subsidies should not necessarily be considered a sign of ineffective operation of SOEs since discrepancy between two subsides could arise as a result of external factors, or there may have been erroneous projections or measurement of either the costs of NCOs or the costs of factors of production. In such circumstances, the SOEs must be reimbursed for the deviation between ex-ante and ex-post subsidies as the result of the projection error. Some variation in costs may be expected whenever a study is within the framework of partial equilibrium analysis.

In our pricing model, the costs of commercial objectives are financed internally by means of markup pricing, and the costs of social objectives are to be met by government subsidies in accordance with the contract plan. For the proper evaluation of the performance of SOEs, we have developed a model–the goal attainment model–where the success or failure of an SOE must be judged on the basis of its goal achievement. In other words, the variation between target goals and attained goals is our primary interest. Because of multiple objectives of SOEs, goals are ranked and assigned weights in accordance with their predetermined priorities. The degree of effectiveness is the ratio of ex-post composite weight and rank to ex-ante composite weight and rank when it is adjusted for the negative impact of contradictory goals. The closer the ratio is to one, the better the degree of effectiveness. In the goal attainment model, we are not concerned with the logic behind the social objectives, but with whether such goals are actually attained. Our model makes a clear distinction between efficiency and effectiveness, the former referring to the ratio of inputs to outputs, and the latter indicating the extent to which the desired objectives have been attained. If SOEs are obligated to attain social objectives, then subsidization should be based on the degree of success in meeting such objectives. In essence, our goal attainment model is a synthesis of our pricing model and the contract plan.

The motives for starting SOEs or taking over stagnating enterprises in most countries, whether developed or developing, have included full industrialization, modernization, solving the problem of economic heterogeneity by removing disparity among regions, or preventing unemployment, rather than merely the efficient allocation of resources. To achieve these developmental objectives, SOEs, either by design or accident, were forced to invest large amounts at considerable risk in less prosperous areas, despite the possibility of losses and without considering either opportunity costs or output values. We concluded that the activities of SOEs are not necessarily based on a profit motive but on national emergencies, structural inadequacies, strategic importance, and social problems. The objective functions for SOEs are more complex than those of private enterprises. We believe that microeconomic intervention by SOEs is necessary in order to achieve macro objectives in a consistent manner. Achieving these objectives through the sacrifice of microeconomic efficiency often entails economic losses. The amount of this sacrifice (i.e., economic loss) might reflect the extent of the SOEs' social obligations (i.e., social profits). Thus, tradeoffs between micro and macro objectives are inevitable and make performance evaluation inaccurate if it is based solely on financial perfomance.

APPENDIX A2.1
Capital Intensity or Output per Unit of Capital

COUNTRY	YEARS	IP/IT / OP/OT	OP/OT / IP/IT
"World" (average)		**1.42**	**.70**
Industrial Countries (average)		**1.15**	**.86**
Australia	(1954-1979)	2.00	.50
Austria	(1970-1979)	1.32	.45
Belgium	(1953-1979) [a]	1.35	.74
Canada	(1970-1980) [a]	1.43	.70
Denmark	(1974)	1.31	.76
Finland	(1970-1975)	1.23	.81
France	(1959-1981)	1.62	.62
Germany	(1962-1979) [b]	1.15	.87
Ireland	(1974-1978) [a]	1.29	.78
Italy	(1967-1980)	2.21	.45
Japan	(1965-1980) [a]	1.29	.77
Netherlands	(1968-1978) [b]	3.84	.26
Norway	(1959-1980) [a]	1.68	.60
Spain	(1974-1980) [a]	1.54	.65
Sweden	(1978-1980) [a]	1.59	.63
United Kingdom	(1962-1981)	1.73	.50
Developing Countries (average)		**3.13**	**.31**
Venezuela	(1972-1980)	1.77	.56
Africa (average)		**1.35**	**.54**
Botswana	(1974-1979)	1.61	.62
Ivory Coast	(1965-1979) [b]	2.87	.35
Kenya	(1964-1979)	1.70	.59
Mali	(1975-1978)	1.38	.72
Sierra Leone	(1979)	2.57	.39
Tanzania	(1966-1977)	2.95	.34
Tunisia	(1967-1981)	1.36	.73
Asia (average)		**3.46**	**.26**
Bangladesh	(1974)	5.44	.18

APPENDIX A2.1 Continued

COUNTRY	YEARS	IP/IT / OP/OT	OP/OT / IP/IT
Burma	(1968-1980)[a]	5.84	.17
India	(1960-1978)	4.97	.20
Korea	(1963-1980)	3.97	.25
Pakistan	(1961-1981)	7.41	.14
Sri Lanka	(1961-1978)[b]	3.08	.32
Taiwan	(1951-1980)	2.45	.41
Greece	(1975-1979)	1.61	.62
Malta	(1962-1980)	2.51	.40
Portugal	(1976-1980)[b]	2.24	.45
Turkey	(1962-1980)	3.15	.32
Western Hemisphere		**3.40**	**.29**
Argentina	(1976-1980)	4.29	.23
Bahamas	(1975-1980)[a]	3.93	.25
Barbados	(1975-1980)	1.59	.63
Bolivia	(1971-1977)	3.60	.28
Chile	(1974-1980)	1.17	.86
Colombia	(1974-1980)[a]	1.45	.69
Guyana	(1973-1980)	1.38	.74
Mexico	(1975-1978)	3.38	.30
Paraguay	(1970-1980)	3.61	.28

Notes:
a: The average percentage share of GDP at factor cost (IP/IT) of industrial and developing countries was used whenever the I_P/I_T for the country under study was not available.
b: If the I_P/I_T was not available for the entire period, the available data were used as an average for capital intensity.

Source: This appendix is derived from "The Role of Public Enterprises: An International Statistical Comparison" in *Public Enterprise in Mixed Economies: Some Macroeconomic Aspects*, R. H. Floyd, C. S. Gray, and R. P. Short, IMF, Washington, D.C., 1984.

APPENDIX A2.2
Percentage Shares of Public Enterprises in the Output or Investment of Major Sectors

	YEARS	A	B	C	D	E	F	G
Industrial Countries								
Australia	(1967-79)[1]	0.23	5.35	3.65	95.20	14.88	0.08	49.25
Austria	(1970-75)[3]	3.00	23.00		78.00[2]	2.00	1.00	78.00[2]
Belgium	(1962-79)[2]	xxx	xxx	0.28	20.84	xxx	xxx	81.42
Finland	(1972-80)[2]	....	....	30.43	....	....	....	....
France	(1971)[2]	xxx	11.40		96.60	xxx	xxx	68.30
Ireland	(1974-77)[2]	....	63.20[b]	9.40	63.20[b]	xxx	xxx	55.60
Italy	(1967-78)[2]	....	22.05	65.30	14.23	3.48	66.20	....
Netherlands	(1970-73)[2]	xxx	xxx	37.00	xxx	xxx	xxx	46.20
U.K.	(1970-81)[2]	xxx	26.03	8.43	92.10	xxx	xxx	54.60
Developing Countries								
Iraq	(1960-75)[2]	....	....	53.40	....	....	....	....
Nigeria	(1970-74)[2]	....	....	....	17.70	....	....	....
Benin	(1975-79)[2]	....	....	57.65	....	....	....	....
Congo	(1976)[4]	3.10[c]	....	15.70	92.60	12.90	....	52.30
Ethiopia	(1974-80)[1]	....	....	50.90	....	....	....	....
Ivory Coast	(1979)[1]	0.10	25.20	....	87.60	12.80	....	35.20
Kenya	(1970-73)[1]	0.40	4.20	13.10	69.00	8.40	2.60	68.70
Morocco	(1973-76)[2]	....	....	17.75	....	....	....	....
Senegal	(1974)[3]	0.90	99.20	19.00	100.00	5.70	23.70	37.80
Sierra Leone	(1979)[1]	5.30	26.10	14.20	91.60	xxx	0.10	8.80
Somalia	(1974-77)[1]	....	....	59.10		....	....	....
Tanzania	(1966-77)[1]	1.96	87.06	28.23	76.66	3.63	13.43	45.03
Tunisia	(1978-81)[2]	18.30	47.30	58.80	89.40	....	....	60.40
Bangladesh	(1974)[1]	xxx	62.00		78.10	2.80	7.50	18.80
Burma	(1980)[3d]	0.50	85.50	56.20	100.00	....	....	45.40
India	(1970-78)[1]	1.90	68.73	15.00	82.73	15.00	4.27	54.66
Korea	(1963-77)[1]	0.23	21.87	13.66	81.96	4.13	1.13	29.47
Nepal	(1971-75)[1]	0.10	....	4.20	43.95	28.75	....	11.70
Pakistan	(1970-75)[1]	xxx	15.25	5.95	78.85	xxx	3.65	34.45
Singapore	(1972)[1]	....	....	14.20	....	....	....	....
Sri Lanka	(1974)[1]	0.50	0.50	33.50	93.50	6.80	10.60	45.60
Taiwan	(1980)[2]	13.40	85.50	31.90	95.90	25.80	11.00	49.50
Thailand	(1970-73)[1]	0.20	0.30	5.20	73.10	xxx	0.30	17.20
Greece	(1979)[1]	xxx	71.40[b]	1.30	71.40[b]	.....	....	42.70
Portugal	(1976)[1]	0.90	4.90	12.00	78.20	xxx	1.00	43.50
Turkey	(1974-77)[2]	15.40	xxx	42.10	xxx	xxx	xxx	23.30

APPENDIX A2.2 Continued

	YEARS	A	B	C	D	E	F	G
Egypt	(1979)[2]	....	80.40		....	....	....	....
Yemen Arab Republic	(1975-76)[2]	....	....	59.50	....	....	....	....
Bolivia	(1973-75)[1]	0.10	85.40	5.90	9.90	0.60	xxx	9.00

Notes:
A: agriculture, hunting, forestry, and fishing
B: mining and quarrying
C: manufacturing
D: electricity, gas, and water
E: construction
F: wholesale and retail trade, restaurants, and hotels
G: transportation, storage, and communications

1: Gross Domestic Product at Factor Cost (GDPF)
2: Gross Domestic Fixed Capital Formation (GFCF)
3: Gross Domestic Product at Market Prices (GDPM)
4: Gross Value of Output (GO)

a: share in electricity, gas, and water plus transportation, storage, and communications
b: share in electricity, gas, and water plus mining and quarrying
c: share in agriculture only
d: share in GDPM at 1970 prices

Source: This appendix is derived from "The Role of Public Enterprises: An International Statistical Comparison" in *Public Enterprises in Mixed Economies: Some Macroeconomic Aspects*, R. H. Floyd, C. S. Gray, and R. P. Short, IMF, Washington, D.C., 1984, pp. 126-129.

APPENDIX A2.3
Industry Coverage of Public Enterprises

	A2/	A3/	A4/	A5/	A6/	A7/	A8/	A9/
				Part A				
Industrial Countries								
Australia			D,T					
Austria	FO	C,P,M					PR	P
Belgium			F					
Canada		P						P
Denmark	FO	P		C				
Finland	A		F	T			PA	P
France		C,P	T					P
Germany, Fed. Rep. of		C	D					P
Ireland	FI	M	S,F					
Italy		C	F,T	T,C			PR	P
Japan			D,T					P
Luxembourg								
Netherlands		C,P						
Norway	FO,FI	C,P	F,D					
Sweden	FO	P,M	T	T		W	PR	P
United Kingdom		C,P						PR
United States								
Developing Countries								
Oil Exporting Countries								
Indonesia	A,FI	C,P,M	S,T	T			PA	P
Nigeria	A,FI	C,P	S,F,D	T			PA	P
Venezuela		P,M	S					P
Africa								
Benin	FO,AD		F,D	T			PR	
Botswana	AD							
Congo	A,FI	M	F,D,T	T		W,F	PR	P
Ethiopia	AD		S,D	T,C	L,F	W	PA,PR	
Gambia, The	FI							
Ghana	AD	M	F,D				PA	
Ivory Coast	AD,FI	P,M	S,F	T	F		PR	P
Kenya	A,FI	M	S,F	T,C				P
Liberia	AD		S,F		F			P
Mali		M	F	T				

APPENDIX A2.3 Continued

	A2/	A3/	A4/	A5/	A6/	A7/	A8/	A9/
Mauritania	A,FI	M		C				
Mauritius	AD		F					
Morocco	AD	P,M	S,F,D,T					P
Niger	AD	M						
Senegal	AD	P,M		T			PR	P
Sierra Leone	FI	M	D			W,F		P
Somalia	FI		D	T	L			P
Tanzania	AD,FI	M	S,F,D,T	T		W	PA,PR	P
Togo	AD,FI	M	F	T				
Tunisia	FI	P,M	S,D,T				PR	P
Upper Volta	A		S	T	F		PR	P
Zambia	A	M	S,F,T	T		W	PR	P
Asia								
Bangladesh	AD,FI	M	S,F,T	T	L	W	PA	P
Burma	A,FO,FI	M	F,D	T		W	PA	P
India	A,FI	C,M	F	T	L		PA	P
Korea	AD,FI	C,M	F,D,T				PR	P
Nepal	A,FO	M	S,T	T	L			
Pakistan	AD	C,P,M	F				PR	P
Papua New Guinea	A		S					
Philippines	AD		T	T				P
Sri Lanka	AD,FI	M	S,F,D,T	T		W	PR	P
Thailand	FO,FI	M	S,F,T	T		W	PA	P
Europe								
Greece			S,T					P
Malta	FI		F	C	F			
Portugal	FI	C,M	S,F,D,T	T		F	PA,PR	P
Turkey	A,FO,FI	C,M	S,F	T			PA	P
Middle East								
Syrian Arab Republic			F,T	T			PR	P
Western Hemisphere								
Argentina	FO	C,P,M	S					P
Bahamas	AD							
Barbados	AD							
Bolivia		P,M						

APPENDIX A2.3 Continued

	A2/	A3/	A4/	A5/	A6/	A7/	A8/	A9/
Brazil	AD,FO	C,M	F				PR	P
Chile		C,M	S					
Colombia	AD	C,M	F		L			P
Costa Rica		M	S,F				PR	P
Dominica	FO							
Dominican Republic		M	S,F	T	L,F		PA	P
Ecuador	A,FI		D					
Guyana	A,FO	M	S,F,D		L,F	F	PA,PR	P
Haiti			F,T	T			PR	
Honduras	FO		S					
Jamaica	AD	M	F	T,C				P
Mexico	A,FO	P,M	S,F	T				P
Panama	A	M	S				PA	
Paraguay								P
Peru		P,M	F					P
St. Lucia								
Uruguay								

	B10/	B11/	B12/	B13/	B*	B¯	B#	B15/
				Part B				
Industrial Countries								
Australia					E	E		T
Austria	PH,C	P	I	A	E	E	C	
Belgium						E		
Canada						E		A
Denmark						E	C	T
Finland	C		I	M		E		
France	C			A	E	E	C	
Germany, Fed. Rep. of	C	P	I,B	M,S		E		T
Ireland	FE,C		I			E	C	
Italy	PH,C	C	I	M,A,S	E	E	C	A,T
Japan						E	C	A
Luxembourg	C					E		
Netherlands	C		I			E		A
Norway	PH,C		I,B			E		T
Sweden	PH,C		I	M,S		E	C	A
United Kingdom			I	M,A,S		E		

APPENDIX A2.3 Continued

	B10/	B11/	B12/	B13/	B*	B'	B#	B15/
United States					E			
Developing Countries Oil Exporting Countries								
Indonesia	PH,FE	P,C	I	M,A,S	E	E	C	T
Nigeria	FE	C	I	M,S	E	E		T
Venezuela	FE,C		I,B			E	C	A,T
Africa								
Benin		P				E		A,T
Botswana					E	E	C	A
Congo		P,C		S		E	C	A,T
Ethiopia	PH,C	P				E	C	A,T
Gambia, The				S		E		A,T
Ghana	PH	P	I		E	E	C	A,T
Ivory Coast	FE	P,C,B				E	C	A,T
Kenya	FE,C			M	E	E	C	A
Liberia						E		
Mali	PH	C,B				E		A,T
Mauritania	PH					E		A
Mauritius						E		A,T
Morocco					E	E		A
Niger		P,C				E	C	A
Senegal	FE					E	C	T
Sierra Leone						E	C	A,T
Somalia		B				E		A,T
Tanzania	PH,FE	C	I	M	E	E		A,T
Togo	PH		I			E	C	A,T
Tunisia	PH,FE	P,C	I,B			E	C	T
Upper Volta		B				E		A,T
Zambia	C	P,C		M	E	E		A,T
Asia								
Bangladesh	PH,FE,C	C	I	M	E	E		T
Burma	C				E	E	C	A,T
India	PH,FE,C	P	I	M,S	E	E		A,T
Korea	FE,C	C	I,B	M	E	E	C	A
Nepal		P,C			E	E	C	A,T
Pakistan	FE,C	C	I	M,S	E	E	C	A,T
Papua New Guinea						E		A

APPENDIX A2.3 Continued

	B10/	B11/	B12/	B13/	B*	B^{-}	B#	B15/
Philippines	FE,C					E		A
Sri Lanka	PH,FE	P,C	I	M	E	E	C	A,T
Thailand	PH	P				E	C	A,T
Europe								
Greece				A	E	E		A,T
Malta				S	E	E		A
Portugal	PH,C	P,C	I	S	E	E	C	A,T
Turkey	C	C	I		E	E		A
Middle East								
Syrian Arab Republic	PH					E		A
Western Hemisphere								
Argentina	C		I	S		E		
Bahamas						E		
Barbados						E		A,T
Bolivia	C	C	I			E		A,T
Brazil	FE,C		I	A,S	E	E		A
Chile	C		I			E		A
Colombia	FE	C		M,A,S		E		A
Costa Rica		C				E		T
Dominica						E		A,T
Dominican Republic	C	P,C		M		E		A
Ecuador	FE		I			E		A,T
Guyana	PH	P,C				E		A
Haiti						E		A,T
Honduras						E		A,T
Jamaica						E		A,T
Mexico	C		I			E	C	T
Panama		C				E		A
Paraguay			I			E		
Peru	C		I	S		E		
St. Lucia						E		A
Uruguay		C				E		T

APPENDIX A2.3 Continued

	Hotels (H)	C16/	C17/	C18/	Housing (HO)
			Part C		
Industrial Countries					
Australia	H	R	A,W	P	
Austria	H	R,B	A,AP,W	P	H
Belgium		R,B	A,P	P	H
Canada		R,B	W,P	P	
Denmark		R,B	A,AP,W,P	P	H
Finland		R,B	A	P	
France		R,B	A,AP,W	P	
Germany, Fed. Rep. of		R	A	P	H
Ireland		R,B	A,AP,W,P	P	
Italy		R,B	A	P	
Japan		R	AP	P	H
Luxembourg		R	AP	P	
Netherlands		R,B	A,AP,W,P	P	
Norway		R	A	P	H
Sweden		R	A	P	H
United Kingdom		R,B	A,AP,W,P	P	
United States		R	AP	P	
Developing Countries					
Oil Exporting Countries					
Indonesia	H	R,B	A,W	P	
Nigeria	H	R	A,AP,W,P	P	
Venezuela	H	R,B	A,AP,W,P	P	
Africa					
Benin	H	R	W,P	P	
Botswana	H			P	H
Congo	H	R,B	A,W,P	P	
Ethiopia	H	R,B	A,W	P	H
Gambia, The	H		A,P	P	
Ghana	H	R,B	A,P	P	H
Ivory Coast	H	R,B	A,P	P	H
Kenya	H	R,B	A,W,P	P	
Liberia			A,AP,W,P	P	H
Mali	H	R,B	A,W	P	

APPENDIX A2.3 Continued

	Hotels (H)	C16/	C17/	C18/	Housing (HO)
Mauritania	H	B	A	P	
Mauritius		B	AP,P	P	H
Morocco	H	R	A,AP,P	P	H
Niger	H	B	A	P	
Senegal	H	R	A,W,P	P	H
Sierra Leone		B	A,AP,W,P	P	
Somalia	H		A,W	P	
Tanzania	H	R	A,W,P	P	
Togo	H	R	A,W,P	P	
Tunisia		R,B	A,AP,W,P	P	H
Upper Volta	H	R	A	P	H
Zambia	H	R,B	A,W	P	H
Asia					
Bangladesh		R,B	W	P	
Burma		R,B	A,W	P	
India	H	R,B	A,AP,W	P	
Korea	H	R	A,W,P	P	H
Nepal		R	A	P	
Pakistan		R,B	A,W	P	
Papua New Guinea			P	P	H
Philippines		R	W,P	P	H
Sri Lanka	H	R	A,W,P	P	
Thailand		R,B	A,AP,W,P	P	H
Greece		R,B	A,P	P	
Malta	H		A,AP,W,P	P	H
Portugal		R,B	A,W,P	P	
Turkey		R	A,AP,W	P	
Middle East					
Syrian Arab Republic			A,AP,P	P	H
Western Hemisphere					
Argentina	H	R	A,W,P	P	H
Bahamas	H		A,P	P	
Barbados	H	B	AP,P	P	H
Bolivia		R	A,AP	P	
Brazil	H	R,B	A,W,P	P	
Chile		R,B	A,P	P	

APPENDIX A2.3 Continued

	Hotels (H)	C16/	C17/	C18/	Housing (HO)
Colombia	H	R,B	W,P	P	
Costa Rica		R,B	W,P	P	
Dominica			P	P	H
Dominican Republic			A,AP,P	P	H
Ecuador		R	AP,W,P	P	
Guyana			A,W,P	P	
Haiti		B	A,AP,P	P	
Honduras		R	P	P	
Jamaica	H	R,B	A,AP,P	P	H
Mexico		R,B	AP	P	H
Panama		R,B		P	
Paraguay		R	A,AP,W,P	P	
Peru		R,B	A,AP,W,P	P	H
St. Lucia	H		P	P	
Uruguay		R	A,P	P	

Notes:
A2/: A-agricultural production; FO-forestry; FI-fishing; AD-agricultural development (enterprises mainly engaged in the promotion of private sector5 production, for example, through the provision of inputs, rather than directly in production).
A3/: C-coal; P-petroleum and natural gas; M-other and general mining and quarrying.
A4/: S-sugar; F-other food and agricultural processing; D-drink; T-tobacco.
A5/: T-textiles; C-clothing.
A6/: L-leather; F-footwear.
A7/: W-wood products; F-furniture.
A8/: PA-paper; PR-printing.
A9/: P-petroleum refining and/or distribution.
B10/: PH-pharmaceuticals; FE-fertilizer; C-other and general chemicals.
B11/: B-bricks; C-cement; P-pottery and glass.
B12/: I-iron and steel; B-other basic metals.
B13:/ M-motor vehicles; A-aircraft; S-shipbuilding.
B*: Other engineering.
B¨: E-electricity, gas and/or water.
B#:Construction.
B15/: A-agricultural marketing; T-other wholesale or retail trade.
H: Hotels
C16/: R-railways; B-bus and other land transport.
C17/: A-airlines; AP-airports; W-water transportation; P-ports.
C18/: P-posts and/or telecommunications.
HO: Housing

APPENDIX A2.3 Continued

Sources: This appendix is derived from "The Role of Public Enterprises: An International Statistical Comparison" in *Public Enterprises in Mixed Economies: Some Macroeconomic Aspects,* R. H. Floyd, C. S. Gray, and R. P. Short, IMF, Washington, D.C., 1984, pp. 130-141.

APPENDIX A3.1
Percentage of Total Sources of Funds Derived from Internal Sources (retained profits and revenue subsidies)

Years	France[a]	Italy[b]	UK[c]	Ireland[d]
1965	*	*	48	*
1966	*	*	*	50
1967	*	37	*	*
1968	*	*	*	53
1969	*	*	*	*
1970	*	*	44	34
1971	*	*	*	40
1972	52	*	*	33
1973	53	*	*	42
1974	36	29	*	*
1975	37	*	34	37
1976	35	*	*	35
1977	39	*	*	32

Notes:
a: 'Enterprises Nationales' (FDES & CNME).
b: Enti di gestione.
c: Nine major nationalized industries.
d: State-sponsored bodies excluding the post office.
*: Not available.

Source: W. Keyser, R. Windle, and R. Stares. *State Business: Public Enterprise in EEC*, Metra Oxford Consulting, Oxford, 1978, p. 161.

APPENDIX A3.2
State-Owned Companies Financing, FIM Millions

	1981	1982	1983
Gross margins	5,844.0	5,237.3	5,599.8
+ Other incomes	-128.7	-195.7	+582.8
- Interest, taxes, and dividends	2,247.2	2,338.8	2,336.1
Financing from operations	3,468.1	2,702.8	3,846.5
- Changes in operating capital	1,975.9	1,757.0	1,985.9
= Fund available for investment	1,492.2	945.8	1,860.6
- Investments	3,047.1	3,096.7	3,317.6
External Financing Requirement	1,554.9	2,150.9	1,457.0
+ Increase in share capital	90.0	170.1	291.6
+ Increase in loans	1,464.9	1,980.7	1,165.4

Source: Advisory Committee, ***State Owned Companies in Finland,*** Advisory Committee on State Owned Companies, Finland, 1983.

APPENDIX A3.3
The Financial Accounts of the Public Corporations in the U.K. from 1972-1982 (Part A covers 1972-1976 and Part B covers 1977-1982)

	1972	1973	1974	1975	1976
	PART A				
Revenue derived from net sales [a]	5333	5890	6911	9782	12420
Revenue net of capital consumption [b]	3856	4216	4735	6946	9023
Wages and salaries [c]	3863	4328	5615	7691	8655
Interest paid [d]	926	1133	1586	1925	2395
Surplus over wages and interest [e]	-933	-1245	-2466	-2670	-2027
National income [f]	50139	58844	67581	84267	10080
Financial deficit over wages and interest as a % of national income [g]	1.86	2.11	2.64	2.16	2.02

	1977	1978	1979	1980	1981	1982
		PART B				
Revenue derived from net sales [a]	14104	15941	17329	20686	22997	25414
Revenue net of capital consumption [b]	10073	11400	12129	14443	13806	18158
Wages and salaries [c]	9534	11098	12754	15102	16075	16959
Interest paid [d]	2537	2507	2801	2877	3213	3818
Surplus over wages and interest [e]	-1978	-2205	-3426	-3539	-5482	-2619
National income [f]	111754	128621	147183	168153	183800	201073
Financial deficit over wages and interest as a % of national income [g]	1.76	1.71	2.32	2.17	2.98	1.30

Notes:
This appendix is derived from National Income and Expenditure, 1983 edition.
a: TR minus (subsidies and purchases of goods and services plus physical increases in stock) which is derived from Table 6.1 operating account, p. 40.
b: Equal to column (1) minus capital consumption of all fixed assets of the public corporation, which is derived from Table 11.5, p. 72.
c and d: Derived from Table 6.1 and 6.2 on p. 40 respectively.
g: Derived from Table 1.1.

Source: Central Statistical Office, *National Income and Expenditure*, Her Majesty's Stationery Office, London, 1983.

APPENDIX A3.4
Internal Funds Before Subsidy and Compensation (percentages)

	1969	1970	1971	1972	1973	1974
British Rail and National Coal Board	30	26	-80	-20	-127	-153
Other Major Nationalized Industries	54	42	51	53	39	27
Nine Major Nationalized Industries	53	41	41	41	24	17

Source: National Economic Development Office, *A Study of U.K. Nationalized Industries*, Appendix B, Her Majesty's Stationery Office, London, 1976, p. 70.

APPENDIX A3.5

Sales, Gross Investments, Pretax Income, Return on Total Assets, and Employees in Sweden, 1979-1981

Statsföretag	1978-1979	1980-1981
Sale M SwKr	12344,4	15,562
Changes in Sales (%)	+20	+10
Sales Outside Sweden % of Total Sales	50	52
Gross Investments in SwKr	1765,0	1844,0
Pretax Income M SwKr	-509,0	-578
Change in Pretax Income M SwKr	+420,4	-839
Return on Total Assets (%)	1.0	2.8
Employees	46,458	46,080

Notes:
a: Sales figures are exclusive of value added taxes and other excess taxes.
b: Sales outside Sweden consists of exports from Sweden plus sales by foreign units less internal deliveries.
c: Pretax income is income after normal depreciation, net financial income or expenses, net currency gains or losses, but before nonrecurring items, year-end adjustments, and taxes.
d: Return on total assets is computed before taxes; it is defined as pretax income plus interest expenses, taken as a percentage of average total assets.

Sources: The figures for 1978-79 are derived from *Swedish Industry Faces the 80s*, M. Hollvarsson, edited and translated by V. Kayfetz, The Federation of Swedish Industries, Stockholm, Sweden, pp. 148-152. The figures for 1980-81 are derived from *Some Data About Sweden 1983-1984*, Skandinaviska, Enskilda Banken, 1983, p. 38.

APPENDIX A3.6
Government Support to Industry in Sweden

Subsidies	420	1593	2594	6224	5230	5080	8430	10500
Loans and Equity Capital	2023	1214	2212	4414	1650	2130	1660	1550

Source: *Some Data About Sweden 1983-1984*, Skandinaviska, Enskilda Banken, New York, 1983, p. 26.

APPENDIX A3.7
Production of Iron Ore in Selected Countries (million metric tons)

	1950	1960	1970	1981
USSR	39.0	106.5	195.5	242.0
Australia	2.4	4.4	51.1	94.5
USA	99.7	90.2	91.2	75.5
Brazil	0.9	5.3	30.0	64.9
Canada	3.3	55.0	43.0	49.7
India	3.0	10.6	31.4	41.2
South Africa	1.2	3.1	9.2	28.3
Sweden	13.6	21.3	31.5	23.2
France	30.0	67.7	57.4	21.6
Venezuela	0.2	19.5	22.0	15.7
Fed. Republic of Germany	10.9	18.9	6.8	1.6
United Kingdom	13.1	17.4	12.0	0.7
World total	**245.0**	**515.0**	**774.0**	**850.0**

Source: Some Data About Sweden 1983-1984, Skandinaviska, Enskilda Banken, New York, 1983, p. 67.

APPENDIX A3.8
Subsidies and Other Current Transfer (as a percentage of GDP at market prices)

	YEARS	
Belgium	(1970-1979)	2.96
Denmark	(1970-1980)	0.66
France	(1959-1980)	0.68
Italy	(1966-1980)	1.25
Netherlands	(1974-1977)	1.00
Norway	(1970-1976)	0.65
Spain	(1970-1979)	0.93
U.K.	(1967-1982)	0.83
Algeria	(1970-1980)	1.73
Indonesia	(1972-1980)	0.83
Venezuela	(1972-1980)	0.63
Tanzania	(1963-1977)	0.30
Tunisia	(1968-1981)	1.65
Zambia	(1965-1980)	2.16
India	(1966-1978)	0.32
Korea	(1972-1980)	0.26
Pakistan	(1973-1981)	0.20
Sri Lanka	(1962-1980)	1.20
Turkey	(1964-1979)	0.98
Mexico	(1975-1978)	0.95

Sources: This appendix, for all countries except the United Kingdom, is derived from "The Role of Public Enterprises: An International Statistical Comparison" in *Public Enterprises in Mixed Economies: Some Macroeconomic Aspects,* R. H. Floyd, C. S. Gray, and R. P. Short, IMF, Washington, D.C., 1984, pp. 168-174. The U.K. figure is derived from *National Income and Expenditure, 1967-1977 and 1983,* Central Statistical Office, Her Majesty's Stationery Office, London.

APPENDIX A3.9

Subsidies as a Percentage of Revenue (1) and as a Percentage of GDP of the U.K. (2)

YEARS	(1)	(2)
1967-1970	2.53	0.46
1971-1974	5.34	0.96
1975-1978	4.56	0.92
1979-1982	3.13	0.99

Sources: This appendix is derived from *National Income and Expenditure 1967-1977 and 1983*, Central Statistical Office, Her Majesty's Stationary Office, London. (1) is derived from Table 6.1 and (2) is derived from Tables 1.1 and 6.1.

APPENDIX A3.10
Capital Write-offs for Some of the Nationalized Industries for Indicated Periods

Date	Industries	Write-offs (pounds)
31 March 1965	National Coal Board	415.0
31 March 1965	BOAC	110.0
31 March 1965	BEA	25.0
31 December 1965	British Rail	1262.1
31 December 1968	British Waterways	15.5
1 January 1970	British Transport	269.8
1 April 1972	British Steel Corporation	350.0
16 March 1973	Post Office	130.6
31 March 1973	National Coal Board	3053.0

Source: Redwood, John. "Government and the Nationalized Industries," *Lloyds Bank Review*, No. 121, April 1976, p. 41.

APPENDIX A3.11
Capital Write-offs and Government Revenue Support for the Major Nationalized Industries (million pounds)

	1963-68	1969-74	1963-74
Revenue subsidies and compensation	853[a]	2565	3418
Write-offs of government loan capital against revenue deficits, etc.	535[a]	2194	2729[a]
Total government financial support of a revenue nature	1388[a]	4759	6147[a]
Internal funding (before subsidies)	3143	4043	7186

Note:
a: Excludes 130 million pounds revenue grants and 487 million pounds capital write-offs in 1963 for British Transport Commission, which are properly attributable to the pre-1963 period.

Source: National Economic Development Office, "*A Study of U.K. Nationalized Industries*," Central Statistical Office, Her Majesty's Stationery Office, London, 1976, p. 71.

APPENDIX A3.12
Percentage Yield for BSC, BA, and NG (millions)

Year End	Issued Value of PDC	Divs paid	Issued Value of PDC	Divs paid	Issued Value of PDC	Divs paid
1971	700.0	-	65.0	4.9	-	-
1972	500.0	-	65.0	3.3	-	-
1973	500.0	-	125.0	4.4	-	-
1974	500.0	15.9	136.3	6.1	-	-
1975	545.0	7.1	216.3	-	-	-
1976	889.5	-	280.0	-	13.0	0.3
1977	889.5	-	290.0	11.0	13.0	1.3
1978	1379.5	-	300.0	-	13.0	0.8
1979	1324.0	-	310.0	15.0	17.0	0.9
1980	1824.0	-	320.0	7.0	17.0	1.2

Source: Lumby, Stephen. "New Ways of Financing Nationalized Industries," *Lloyds Bank Review*, No. 141, July 1981, p. 39.

APPENDIX A3.13
Foreign and Domestic Borrowing (i.e., Central Government, Banking System, and Other Domestic Borrowing) for Financing the Deficit (as a percentage of total financing)

	Years	Foreign	Domestic
"World" (average)		**25.64**	**74.35**
Norway	(1969-1976)	44.87	55.12
Spain	(1979-1980)	16.12	83.87
Botswana	(1978-1979)	66.66	33.33
Guinea	(1976-1979)	1.27	98.72
Tanzania	(1966-1975)	36.00	63.47
India	(1966-1978)	0.00	100.00
Korea	(1963-1980)	34.14	64.87
Thailand	(1969-1979)	63.82	35.74
Portuga	(1978-1980)	35.80	64.19
Turkey	(1966-1980)	14.49	85.50
Bolivia	(1974-1977)	72.72	27.27
Brazil	(1980)	47.05	52.94
Dominican Republic	(1975-1979)	78.94	21.05
Haiti	(1976-1980)	65.51	34.48
Honduras	(1978-1979)	56.52	43.47
Paraguay	(1970-1980)	94.00	6.00
Peru	(1968-1979)	78.02	23.07
Sri Lanka	(1975-1979)	35.13	64.86

Source: This appendix is derived from Table 6 of "The Role of Public Enterprises: An International Statistical Comparison" in *Public Enterprise in Mixed Economies: Some Macroeconomic Aspects*, R. H. Floyd, C. S. Gray, and R. P. Short, IMF, Washington, D.C., 1984, pp. 162-165.

APPENDIX A4.1
Total Financing (a) and Investment Output Shares of Public Enterprises

COUNTRY	YEARS	TF	$\frac{IP/IT}{OP/OT}$
Spain	(1979-1980)	3.10	3.92
Botswana	(1978-1979)	0.60	1.61
Tanzania	(1966-1975)	2.30	2.95
India	(1966-1978)	5.25	3.72
Korea	(1963-1980)	4.10	3.96
Thailand	(1969-1979)	1.18	2.72
Turkey	(1966-1980)	5.18	3.43
Argentina	(1976-1977)	3.10	4.31
Bolivia	(1971-1977)	3.90	3.60
Chile	(1974-1980)	0.30	1.16
Paraguay	(1970-1980)	1.25	3.60

Note:
a: Total Financing = Domestic plus Foreign Sources of Financing.

Source: This appendix is derived from "The Role of Public Enterprises: An International Statistical Comparison" in *Public Enterprise in Mixed Economies: Some Macroeconomic Aspects*, R. H. Floyd, C. S. Gray, and R. P. Short, IMF, Washington, D.C., 1984, Table 1, p. 120 and Table 6, p. 162.

APPENDIX A4.2
Domestic Borrowing and Investment Output Ratio of Public Enterprises

COUNTRY	YEARS	DB	IP/IT / OP/OT
Norway	(1970-1980)	0.90	1.93
Botswana	(1978-1979)	0.20	1.05
Tanzania	(1966-1973)	0.90	3.22
India	(1966-1978)	5.25	3.76
Korea	(1963-1980)	2.66	3.96
Thailand	(1969-1973)	0.45	2.63
Portugal	(1978-1980)	5.20	3.53
Turkey	(1964-1980)	4.43	3.15
Bahamas	(1975-1979)	2.00	2.76
Bolivia	(1974-1977)	1.20	3.38
Brazil	(1980)	0.90	2.42
Chile	(1974-1980)	-0.25	1.16
Colombia	(1974-1976)	-0.20	2.04
Dominica	(1975-1979)	-0.55	1.77
Dominican Republic	(1975-1979)	0.20	1.12
Haiti	(1976-1980)	0.50	1.52
Honduras	(1978-1979)	1.00	1.55
Jamaica	(1976-1980)	3.75	3.42
Paraguay	(1970-1980)	0.08	3.60
Peru	(1968-1979)	0.53	1.56
St. Lucia	(1975-1979)	2.40	1.01

Source: This appendix is derived from "The Role of Public Enterprises: An International Statistical Comparison" in *Public Enterprise in Mixed Economies: Some Macroeconomic Aspects*, R. H. Floyd, C. S. Gray, and R. P. Short, IMF, Washington, D.C., 1984, Table 1, p.120 and Table 6, p.162.

APPENDIX A4.3
Foreign Borrowing and Investment Output Ratio of Public Enterprises

COUNTRY	YEARS	FB	$\frac{IP/IT}{OP/OT}$
Norway	(1969-1979)	0.70	1.61
Spain	(1979-1980)	0.50	3.92
Algeria	(1970-1980)	8.10	7.18
Botswana	(1978-1979)	0.40	1.05
Ivory Coast	(1975-1980)	2.15	3.38
Tanzania	(1966-1973)	0.90	3.22
Tunisia	(1976-1977)	4.50	1.53
India	(1966-1978)	0.00	3.76
Korea	(1963-1980)	1.44	3.96
Thailand	(1969-1979)	0.75	2.72
Portugal	(1978-1980)	2.90	2.32
Turkey	(1966-1980)	0.75	3.43
Argentina	(1976-1980)	1.10	4.28
Bahamas	(1975-1979)	-0.02	3.93
Bolivia	(1974-1977)	3.20	3.38
Brazil	(1980)	0.80	3.45
Chile	(1974-1980)	0.55	1.17
Colombia	(1974-1976)	0.90	3.47
Dominica	(1975-1979)	3.35	2.52
Dominican Republic	(1975-1979)	0.75	1.47
Haiti	(1976-1980)	0.95	2.17
Honduras	(1978-1979)	1.30	2.21
Paraguay	(1970-1980)	1.18	3.60
Peru	(1968-1979)	1.76	2.24
St. Lucia	(1975-1979)	1.30	1.43
Uruguay	(1976-1980)	0.90	2.46

Source: This appendix is derived from "The Role of Public Enterprises: An International Statistical Comparison" in ***Public Enterprise in Mixed Economies: Some Macroeconomic Aspects***, R. H. Floyd, C. S. Gray, and R. P. Short, IMF, Washington, D.C., 1984, Table 1, p. 120 and Table 6, p. 162.

APPENDIX A4.4
Budgetary Burden and Investment Shares of Public Enterprises

COUNTRY	YEARS	BB_{pe}	IP/IT
Australia	(1973-1980)	0.07	18.72
Belgium	(1970-1979)	2.80	12.70
Italy	(1970-1980)	3.40	17.05
Netherlands	(1974-1977)	0.00	14.10
Norway	(1969-1977)	1.73	15.53
Spain	(1974-1979)	1.27	14.46
United Kingdom	(1946-1981)	1.16	18.67
Algeria	(1970-1980)	18.13	61.67
Venezuela	(1972-1980)	1.03	26.86
Kenya	(1966-1976)	0.95	13.90
Malawi	(1970-1978)	2.10	26.23
Sierra Leone	(1979)	0.70	19.60
Tanzania	(1963-1977)	2.23	27.60
Tunisia	(1968-1981)	2.93	34.95
Zambia	(1972-1980)	10.10	55.45
India	(1966-1978)	4.23	31.55
Korea	(1974-1980)	0.40	23.95
Pakistan	(1974-1981)	3.20	40.46
Sri Lanka	(1962-1977)	3.65	21.08
Thailand	(1969-1979)	0.33	9.80
Turkey	(1966-1980)	2.10	22.75
Argentina	(1970-1980)	1.80	19.00
Bahamas	(1975-1979)	2.50	26.00
Barbados	(1975-1980)	3.80	10.50
Bolivia	(1974-1977)	-0.40	40.90
Colombia	(1974-1980)	0.20	9.60
Chile	(1974-1980)	-1.15	16.45
Dominican Republic	(1971-1979)	1.26	10.56
Guatemala	(1975-1980)	1.70	12.25
Guyana	(1974-1980)	2.65	36.70
Mexico	(1975-1979)	1.90	28.20
Jamaica	(1976-1979)	2.65	32.15
Panama	(1970-1979)	1.63	24.40
Paraguay	(1970-1980)	0.36	10.46
Peru	(1974-1979)	0.75	-18.48
St. Lucia	(1975-1979)	1.50	9.50

APPENDIX A4.4 Continued

Source: This appendix is derived from"The Role of Public Enterprises: An International Statistical Comparison" in *Public Enterprise in Mixed Economies: Some Macroeconomic Aspects,* R. H. Floyd, C. S. Gray, and R. P. Short, IMF, Washington, D.C., 1984, Table 1, p. 120 and Table 7, p. 168.

APPENDIX A4.5
Capital Account Surplus and Investment Shares of Public Enterprises

COUNTY	YEARS	KD_{pe}	IP/IT
Australia	(1966-1977)	-4.90	18.50
Canada	(1970-1980)	-3.20	13.73
Finland	(1970-1975)	-3.75	11.85
France	(1959-1974)	-5.22	19.50
Italy	(1970-1980)	-3.10	17.05
Japan	(1970-1980)	-3.70	10.96
Netherlands	(1968-1980)	-3.45	13.83
Norway	(1968-1980)	-2.83	17.20
United Kingdom	(1946-1981)	-3.06	18.67
United States	(1967-1978)	-0.83	4.45
Venezuela	(1972-1980)	-8.50	26.86
Botswana	(1974-1979)	-4.50	12.10
Ivory Coast	(1965-1979)	-6.58	30.18
Malawi	(1970-1978)	-6.20	26.23
Mali	(1975-1978)	-2.65	14.25
Tanzania	(1966-1973)	-3.90	35.45
Burma	(1968-1980)	-6.33	46.73
India	(1966-1978)	-6.68	31.53
Korea	(1963-1980)	-6.00	25.00
Taiwan	(1951-1980)	-6.97	32.18
Thailand	(1969-1979)	-2.33	9.80
Turkey	(1966-1980)	-5.98	22.75
Argentina	(1968-1980)	-3.92	18.28
Bahamas	(1975-1980)	-3.05	26.00
Barbados	(1975-1980)	-2.25	10.50
Bolivia	(1971-1977)	-6.40	40.20
Chile	(1974-1980)	-2.50	16.45
Colombia	(1974-1980)	-1.55	9.60
Dominica	(1975-1979)	-4.80	16.65
Dominican Republic	(1971-1979)	-2.00	10.56
Guatemala	(1975-1980)	-2.25	12.25
Guyana	(1973-1980)	-8.23	33.33
Haiti	(1976-1980)	-2.25	14.35
Jamaica	(1976-1980)	-4.40	32.15
Mexico	(1975-1978)	-4.95	28.20
Panama	(1960-1979)	-2.66	15.30
Paraguay	(1970-1980)	-2.46	10.46
Peru	(1968-1979)	-2.48	13.90

APPENDIX A4.5 Continued

Source: This appendix is derived from "The Role of Public Enterprises: An International Statistical Comparison" in *Public Enterprise in Mixed Economies: Some Macroeconomic Aspects*, R. H. Floyd, C. S. Gray, and R. P. Short, IMF, Washington, D.C., 1984, Table 1, p. 120 and Table 5, p. 151.

APPENDIX A4.6

Deficit of Central Government and Subsidies to Public Enterprise (as a percentage of GDP at market prices)

COUNTRY	YEARS	D_{cg}	S_{pe}
Norway	(1969-1976)	2.55	0.65
United Kingdom	(1946-1981)	1.95	0.40
Venezuela	(1972-1980)	0.85	0.61
India	(1966-1978)	4.10	0.43
Turkey	(1966-1977)	2.16	0.55
Bahamas	(1975-1980)	0.80	0.60
Barbados	(1975-1980)	4.75	1.15
Dominican Republic	(1972-1979)	1.40	0.46
Guyana	(1974-1980)	19.20	1.10
Jamaica	(1976-1980)	15.20	0.70
Mexico	(1975-1978)	3.90	0.95
Panama	(1970-1979)	7.36	0.20
St. Lucia	(1975-1979)	2.80	0.40

Source: This appendix is derived from 'The Role of Public Enterprises: An International Statistical Comparison" in *Public Enterprise in Mixed Economies: Some Macroeconomic Aspects*, R. H. Floyd, C. S. Gray, and R. P. Short, IMF, Washington, D.C., 1984, Table 5, p. 151 and Table 7, p. 168.

APPENDIX A4.7
Deficit of Central Government and Budgetary Burden of Public Enterprises (as a percentage of GDP at market prices)

COUNTRY	YEARS	D_{cg}	BB_{pe}
Australia	(1973-1980)	2.56	0.07
Belgium	(1970-1979)	5.13	2.80
Denmark	(1970-1980)	1.60	0.83
France	(1974-1980)	0.70	2.20
Italy	(1966-1980)	6.28	3.10
Netherlands	(1974-1980)	2.20	0.00
Norway	(1969-1976)	1.63	1.73
Spain	(1970-1979)	1.73	1.26
United Kingdom	(1946-1981)	1.73	1.16
Algeria	(1970-1980)	8.56	18.13
Indonesia	(1972-1980)	2.36	3.30
Venezuela	(1972-1980)	0.86	1.03
Ethiopia	(1978-1980)	0.86	1.03
Kenya	(1962-1976)	3.42	0.76
Liberia	(1977-1980)	6.20	2.80
Malawi	(1967-1978)	6.55	1.70
Sierra Leone	(1979)	7.30	0.70
Tanzania	(1963-1977)	4.88	2.23
Tongo	(1978-1980)	3.60	3.80
Tunisia	(1968-1981)	3.85	2.93
Zambia	(1965-1980)	9.30	8.85
Bangladesh	(1979-1981)	11.00	6.00
India	(1966-1978)	4.10	4.23
Korea	(1972-1980)	1.63	0.23
Pakistan	(1973-1981)	7.40	2.36
Papua, New Guinea	(1974-1977)	3.10	1.50
Sri Lanka	(1962-1980)	7.46	5.18
Thailand	(1969-1979)	2.90	0.25
Portugal	(1978-1980)	10.40	2.20
Turkey	(1964-1979)	2.54	1.86
Egypt	(1975-1979)	16.20	2.20
Argentina	(1970-1983)	4.98	1.80
Bahamas	(1975-1980)	0.80	2.50
Barbados	(1975-1980)	4.75	3.80
Bolivia	(1972-1977)	0.85	0.05
Dominican Republic	(1972-1977)	1.40	1.26
Guatemala	(1970-1979)	1.80	1.30

APPENDIX A4.7 Continued

COUNTRY	YEARS	D_{cg}	BB_{pe}
Guyana	(1971-1980)	16.96	2.23
Jamaica	(1976-1979)	15.20	2.65
Mexico	(1975-1978)	4.40	1.90
Panama	(1970-1979)	7.36	1.63
Peru	(1972-1979)	1.43	0.76
St. Lucia	(1975-1979)	2.80	1.50
Uruguay	(1976-1979)	1.05	0.55

Source: This appendix is derived from"The Role of Public Enterprises: An International Statistical Comparison" in *Public Enterprise in Mixed Economies: Some Macroeconomic Aspects*, R. H. Floyd, C. S. Gray, and R. P. Short, IMF, Washington, D.C., 1984, Table 7, p. 168.

APPENDIX A4.8
Growth in Credit and Investment Output Ratio of Public Enterprises

COUNTRY	YEARS	C_g	$\frac{IP/IT}{OP/OT}$
Norway	(1977-1981)	17.15	2.07
Gambia	(1978-1980)	62.40	2.16
Guinea	(1979)	12.00	1.30
Ivory Coast	(1974-1979)	35.50	3.38
Mali	(1975-1978)	20.15	1.38
Burma	(1978-1980)	77.00	7.58
Pakistan	(1976-1981)	32.35	5.50
Greece	(1975-1979)	24.00	1.45
Turkey	(1962-1977)	23.45	2.73
Bolivia	(1974-1977)	74.00	3.38
Guyana	(1973-1980)	36.60	1.37
Haiti	(1976-1980)	34.90	2.17
Peru	(1966-1977)	47.36	2.07

Source: This appendix is derived from"The Role of Public Enterprises: An International Statistical Comparison" in *Public Enterprise in Mixed Economies: Some Macroeconomic Aspects*, R. H. Floyd, C. S. Gray, and R. P. Short, IMF, Washington, D.C., 1984, Table 8, p. 177.

APPENDIX A4.9
Share in Total Domestic Credit and Investment Output Ratio of Public Enterprises

COUNTRY	YEARS	CP/CT	$\frac{IP/IT}{OP/OT}$
Ivory Coast	(1973-1979)	25.76	3.17
Malawi	(1975-1978)	14.86	1.64
Mali	(1975-1978)	34.90	1.38
Mauritania	(1975-1979)	11.43	1.95
Burma	(1977-1980)	49.05	6.25
Greece	(1975-1979)	6.65	1.61
Portugal	(1976-1980)	23.70	2.24
Turkey	(1962-1977)	7.66	2.73
Bolivia	(1973-1977)	26.00	3.60
Guyana	(1974-1980)	18.10	1.22
Haiti	(1976-1980)	18.10	2.17
Peru	(1966-1977)	13.33	2.07

Source: This appendix is derived from "The Role of Public Enterprises: An International Statistical Comparison" in *Public Enterprise in Mixed Economies: Some Macroeconomic Aspects*, R. H. Floyd, C. S. Gray, and R. P. Short, IMF, Washington, D.C., 1984, Table 1, p. 120 and Table 8, p. 177.

Bibliography

Advisory Committee, 1983, *State-Owned Companies in Finland,* Advisory Commitee on State-Owned Companies, Helsingfors, Finland.

Aharoni, Y., 1981, "Managerial Discretion," in *State-Owned Enterprises in the Western Economies;* edited by R. Vernon and Y. Aharoni; St. Martin's Press, New York.

______ 1986, *The Evolution and Management of State-Owned Enterprises,* Ballinger Publishing Company, Cambridge, Massachusetts.

Ahmad, Z. A., ed., 1980, *Financial Profitability and Losses in Public Enterprises of Developing Countries,* International Center for Public Enterprises in Developing Countries, Ljubljana, Yugoslavia.

Alchian, A. A., 1965, "Some Economics of Property Rights," *Politico,* Vol. 30, No. 4, pp. 816-829.

Allen, K., 1972, "Regional Intervention," in *The State as Entrepreneur;* edited by S. Holland, International Arts and Sciences Press, Inc., White Plains, New York.

Altman, E. I., 1971, "Railroad Bankruptcy Propensity," *Journal of Finance,* Vol. 26, No. 2, pp. 333-345.

Anastassopoulos, J. P., 1981, "The French Experience: Conflicts with Government," in *State-Owned Enterprises in the Western Economies;* edited by R. Vernon and Y. Aharoni, St. Martin's Press, New York.

Arrow, K. J., 1964, "The Role of Securities in the Optimal Allocation of Risk-Bearing," *Review of Economic Studies,* Vol. 31, No. 1, pp. 91-96.

______ 1981, "On Finance and Decision Making," in *State-OwnedEnterprises in the Western Economies;* edited by R. Vernon and Y. Aharoni, St. Martin's Press, New York.

______ and R. Lind, 1970, "Uncertainty and Evaluation of Public Investment Decisions," *American Economic Review,* Vol. 60, No. 3, pp. 364-378.

Atkinson, A. B., and J. E. Stiglitz, 1980, *Lectures on Public Economics,* McGraw-Hill Book Company, New York.

Bailey, E. E., and A. F. Friedlaender, 1982, "Market Structure and Multiproduct Industries," *Journal of Economic Literature,* Vol. 20, No. 3, pp. 1024-1048.

Baily, M. J., and M. E. Jensen, 1972, "Risk and the Discount Rate for Public Investment," in *Studies in the Theory of Capital Markets;* edited by M. C. Jensen, Praeger, New York.

Bates, R., and N. Fraser, 1974, *Investment Decisions in Nationalized Fuel Industries,* Cambridge University Press, London, England.

Baumol, W. J., 1965, *Welfare Economics and the Theory of the State,* London School of Economics, London, England.

______ 1968, "On the Social Rate of Discount," *American Economic Review,* Vol. 58, No.4, pp. 788-802.

______ 1980, ed., *Public and Private Enterprise in a Mixed Economy,* St. Martin's Press, New York.

_____ 1982, "Contestable Markets: An Uprising in the Theory of Industry Structure," *American Economic Review*, Vol. 72, No. 1, pp. 1-15.
_____ and D. F. Bradford, 1970, "Optimal Departures from Marginal Cost Pricing," *American Economic Review*, Vol. 60, No. 3, pp. 265-283.
_____ J. Panzar, and R. Willig, 1982, *Contestable Markets and the Theory of Industry Structure*, Harcourt Brace Jovanovich, San Diego, California.
Beesley, M. E., and C. D. Foster, 1965, "The Victoria Line: Social Benefit and Finances," *Journal of the Royal Statistical Society*, Series A, Vol. 128, Part 1, pp. 67-88.
Berczi, A., 1978, "Improving Public Sector Management Through Systematic Measurement of Operational Performance," *Management International Review*, New Series, Vol. 18, No. 2, pp. 63-76.
Bergson, A., 1972, "Optimal Pricing for a Public Enterprise," *Quarterly Journal of Economics*, Vol. 86, No. 2, pp. 519-544.
Blattiner, N., 1981, *Multiproduct Transportation Cost Functions: Scale and Scope in Railway Operations*, University of Basle, Basle, Switzerland.
Boiteux, M., 1971, "On Management of Public Monopolies Subject to Budgetary Constraints," *Journal of Economic Theory*, Vol. 3, No. 3, pp. 219-240.
Borcherding, T. E., W. W. Pommerehne, and F. Schneider, 1982, "Comparing the Efficiency of Private and Public Production: The Evidence from Five Countries," in Public Production; edited by D. Bös, R. A. Musgrave, and J. Wiseman, *Zeitschrift für Nationalökonomie*, Supplementum 2, Springer-Verlag, Vienna, pp. 127-156.
Bös, D., 1981, *Economics Theory of Public Enterprise*, Springer-Verlag, Berlin.
_____ 1986, *Public Enterprise Economics*, North Holland Publishing Company, Amsterdam.
_____ and G. Tillman, 1981, Cost-axiomatic Versus Welfare-Maximizing Marginal Cost Pricing, Mimeo, Institute of Economics, University of Bonn, Bonn.
Bradford, D. F., 1975, "Constraints on Government Investment Opportunities and the Choice of a Discount Rate," *American Economic Review*, Vol. 65, No. 5, pp. 887-899.
Brown, C. V., and P. M. Jackson, 1978, *Public Sector Economies*, Martin Robertson, Oxford, England.
Brown, D. J., and C. R. Heal, 1980, "Two-Part Tariffs, Marginal Cost Pricing and Increasing Returns in a General Equilibrium Model," *Journal of Public Economics*, Vol. 13, No. 1, pp. 25-49
Burn, D., ed., 1958, *The Structure of British Industry*, Cambridge University Press, Cambridge, England.
Cairncross, A. K., 1958, The Pattern of Fixed Capital Investment in Britain, *Westminster Bank Review*, February, pp. 4-8.
Cassese, S., 1981, "Public Control and Corporate Efficiency," in *State-Owned Enterprises in Western Economies;* edited by R. Vernon and Y. Aharoni, St. Martin's Press, New York.

Caves, D. W., and L. R. Christensen, 1980, "The Relative Efficiency of Public and Private Firms in a Competitive Environment: The Case of Canadian Railroads," *Journal of Political Economy*, Vol. 88, No. 5, pp. 958-976.
Central Statistical Office, 1983, *National Income and Expenditure*, Her Majesty's Stationery Office, London, England.
Choksi, M. A., 1979, "State Intervention in the Industrialization of Developing Countries: Selected Issues", Staff Working Papers, No. 34, World Bank, Washington, D.C.
Chu, K., and A. Feltenstein, 1978, "Relative Price Distortions and Inflation: The Case of Argentina 1963-76," International Monetary Fund, Staff Papers, Vol. 25, No. 3, Washington, D.C.
Clifton, J. A., 1983, "Administered Prices in the Context of Capitalist Development," *Contributions to Political Economy*, Vol. 2, pp. 23-38.
Coase, R. H., 1946, "The Marginal Cost Controversy," *Economica*, New Series, Vol. 13, No. 51, pp. 169-182.
Colas, S., 1980, "The Role of Growth of Real Wages and the Role of the State in the Economy," in *Public and Private Enterprise in a Mixed Economy*; edited by W. J. Baumol, St. Martin's Press, New York.
Cook, P., and C. Kirkpatrick, 1988, *Privatization in Less Developed Countries*, St.Martin's Press, New York.
Coopers and Lybrand Associates, 1976, "Review of Pricing Policies, Investment Criteria and Financial Objectives of Four Nationalized Industries," Her Majesty's Stationery Office, London, England.
Cowing, T. G., and A. G. Holtman, 1981, "Multiproduct Short Run Hospital Cost Functions: Empirical Evidence and Policy Implications from Cross-sectional Data," Unpublished Working Paper, SUNY Binghamton, New York.
Day, A., 1963, *Roads*, Mayflower Books, London, England.
Dennsion, S. R., 1958, Investment in the Nationalized Industries, Transactions of the Manchester Statistical Society, Manchester, England, pp. 1-27.
Diamond, P. A., and J. A. Mirrlees, 1971, "Optimal Taxation and Public Production I: Production Efficiency," *American Economic Review*, Vol. 61, No. 1, pp. 8-27.
Dreyfus, P., 1980, "The Efficiency of Public Enterprise: Lessons of French Experience," in *Public and Private Enterprise in a Mixed Economy*; edited by W. J. Baumol, St. Martin's Press, New York.
Dryden, M. M., 1964, "Capital Budgeting: Treatment of Uncertainty and Investment Criteria," *Scottish Journal of Political Economy*, Vol. 11, No. 3, pp. 235-260.
Earl, P., 1983, *The Economic Imagination*, M. E. Sharp, Inc., Armonk, NewYork.
Eichner, A., 1973, "A Theory of the Determination of the Mark-up Under Oligopoly," *Economic Journal*, Vol. 83, No. 332, pp. 1184-1200.
______ 1976, *Megacorp and Oligopoly: Micro Foundation of Macro Dynamics*, Cambridge University Press, Cambridge, England.
______ 1983, "The Micro Foundations of the Corporate Economy," *Managerial and Decision Economics*, Vol. 4, No. 3, pp. 136-152.

Eltis, W., 1979, "The True Deficits of the Public Corporations," *Lloyds Bank Review*, No. 131, Jan., pp. 1-20.

Faulhaber, G. R., 1975, "Cross-Subsidization: Pricing in Public Enterprise," *American Economic Review*, Vol. 65, No. 5, pp. 966-977.

Feldstein, M. S., 1964, "The Social Time Preference and Discount Rate in Cost-Benefit Analysis," *Economic Journal*, Vol. 74, No. 300, pp. 360-379.

_____ 1972, "Equity and Efficiency in Public Sector Pricing: The Optimal Two-Part Tariff," *Quarterly Journal of Economics*, Vol. 86, No. 2, pp. 175-186.

Fleming, J. M., 1944, "Price and Output Policy of State Enterprise," *Economic Journal*, Vol. 55, No. 215, pp. 321-339.

Fleming, J. S., 1977, "What Discount Rate for Public Expenditure?" in *Public Expenditure Allocation Between Competing Ends;* edited by M. V. Posner, Cambridge University Press, Cambridge, England.

Floyd, R. H., 1983, "Some Topical Issues Concerning Public Enterprises," International Monetary Fund, Washington, D.C.

_____ C. S. Gray, and R. P. Short, 1984, *Public Enterprise in Mixed Economies: Some Macroeconomic Aspects*, International Monetary Fund, Washington, D.C.

Fortune, 1981, The Second 500, Vol. 103, pp. 196-224.

Friedman, M., and R. Friedman, 1980, *Free to Choose: A Personal Statement*, Harcourt Brace Jovanovich, New York.

Frisch, R., 1939, "The Dupuit Taxation Theorem," *Econometrica*, Vol. 7, No. 2, pp. 145-150.

Fromm, G., 1981, *Regulation of the Multiproduct Firm: The Case of Telecommunications in Canada*, MIT Press, Cambridge, Massachusetts.

Fung, K. K., 1982, *Social Needs Versus Economic Efficiency in China*, M. E. Sharp, Armonk, New York.

Fuss, M. A., and L. Waverman, 1981, "Regulation of the Multiproduct Firm: The Case of Telecommunications in Canada," in *Studies in Public Regulation;* edited by G. Fromm, MIT Press, Cambridge, Massachusetts, pp. 277-313.

Gassler, R. S., 1986, *The Economics of Nonprofit Enterprise: A Study in Applied Economic Theory*, University Press of America, New York.

Gillis, M., 1977, "Efficiency in State-Owned Enterprises: Selected Cases in Mining from Asia and Latin America," Harvard Institute for International Development, Discussion Paper, No. 27, April.

_____ 1982, "Allocative and X-Efficiency in State-Owned Enterprises: Comparisons Between Bolivia and Indonesia," *Journal of Comparative Economics*, Vol. 6, No. 1, pp. 1-23.

_____ G. P. Jenkins, and D. R. Lessard, 1982, "Public Enterprise Finance: Toward a Synthesis," in *Public Enterprise in Less Developed Countries;* edited by L. P. Jones, Cambridge University Press, Cambridge, Massachusetts.

Gordone, M., 1981, *Government in Business*, Howe Institute, Montreal.

Gough, I., 1979, *The Political Economy of the Welfare State*, Macmillan Press, London, England.

Gould, J. P., and E. P. Lazear, 1989, *Microeconomic Theory*, Richard D. Irwin, Inc., Homewood, Illinois.
Granick, D., 1976, "The Internalizing Externalities in Socialist Enterprise and in Sub Units of Large American Firms," in *Public Enterprise: Economic Analysis of Theory and Practice;* edited by W. G. Shepherd, Lexington Books, Lexington, Massachusetts.
Grant, W., 1982, *The Political Economy of Industrial Policy*, Butterworth Publishers, London, England.
Grassini, F. A., 1981, "The Italian Experience: The Political Constraints," in *State-Owned Enterprise in the Western Economies;* edited by R. Vernon and Y. Aharoni, St. Martin's Press, New York.
Gray, C. S., 1983, "Towards a Conceptual Framework for Macro-Economics Evaluation of Public Enterprise Performance in Mixed Economies," International Monetary Fund, Washington, D.C.
Greece, A., and G. C. Mainiatis, 1967, "Quantitative vs. Qualitative Standards for Evaluating Managerial Efficiency," *Indian Economics Journal*, Vol. 14, No. 5, pp. 576-589.
Hallvarsson, M., 1981, *Swedish Industry Faces the 80s*, The Federation of Swedish Industries, Stockholm, Sweden.
Hanson, A., ed., 1968, *Organization and Administration of Public Enterprise*, United Nations, New York.
Harcourt, G. C., 1982, "The Sraffian Contribution: An Evaluation," in *Classical and Marxian Political Economy;* edited by I. Bradley and M. Howard, Macmillan Press, London, England.
Haririan, M., 1988, "Empirical Evidence for Operating Surplus, Capital Requirements and Debt in State-Owned Enterprises," *Central State Business Review*, Vol. 7, No. 1, pp. 14-17.
Harrod, R., 1958, *Policy Against Inflation*, Macmillan Press, New York.
Hartley, K., 1977, *Problems of Economic Policy*, Allen and Unwin, London.
Hayward, J., 1986, *The State and the Market Economy: Industrial Patriotism and Economic Intervention in France*, New York University Press, New York.
Heald, D., 1980, "The Economic and Financial Control of U.K. Nationalized Industries," *Economic Journal*, Vol. 90, No. 358, pp. 243-265.
Heath, J. B., 1978, "Risk, Return and the Control of Nationalized Industries," Select Committee of Nationalized Industries, London, England, pp. 118-127.
Hemming, R., and A. M. Mansoor, 1988, "Privatization and Public Enterprises," International Monetary Fund, Occasional Paper No. 56, Washington, D.C.
Henderson, J. M., and R. E. Quandt, 1971, *Microeconomic Theory: A Mathematical Approach*, McGraw-Hill Book Company, New York.
Henderson, P. D., 1968, "Investment Criteria for Public Enterprise," in *Public Enterprise: Selected Readings;* edited by R. Turvey, Penguin Books, Baltimore, Maryland.
Hirschleifer, J., 1964, "Efficient Allocation of Capital in an Uncertain World," *American Economic Review*, Vol. 54, No. 3, pp. 77-85.

_____ 1966, "Investment Decision Under Uncertainty: Applications of the State-Preference Approach," *Quarterly Journal of Economics,* Vol. 80, No. 319, pp. 252-276.

Holland, S., 1974, "Europe's New Public Enterprises," in *Big Business and State: Changing Relations in Western Europe;* edited by R. Vernon, Harvard University Press, Cambridge, Massachusetts.

_____ ed., 1972, *The State as Entrepreneur, New Dimensions for Public Enterprise,* International Arts and Sciences Press, Inc., New York.

Holmes, P. M., 1978, *Industrial Pricing,* Macmillan Press, New York.

Holzer, M., ed., 1976, *Productivity in Public Organization,* Kennikat Press, Port Washington, New York.

Hotelling, H., 1938, "The General Welfare in Relation to Problems of Taxation and Railway and Utility Rates," *Econometrica,* Vol. 6, No. 3, pp. 242-269.

Houssiaux, J., 1969, "Consistency of Action: The Comparability of Decision Making by Private and Public Enterprises," in *Public Economics;* edited by M. and H. Guittan, Macmillan Press, New York.

Houthakker, H., 1979, *The Multinational Corporation: A Radical Approach,* Cambridge University Press, Cambridge, England.

International Monetary Fund, 1974, *Draft Manual on Government Finance Statistics,* Washington, D.C.

_____ 1980, *Government Finance Statistics Year Book,* Washington, D.C.

_____ 1986, *A Manual on Government Finance Statistics,* Washington, D.C.

Jara-Diaz, S., and C. Winston, 1981, "Multiproduct Transportation Cost Functions: Scale and Scope in Railway Operations," in Eighth European Association for Research in Industrial Economics, Vol. 1; edited by N. Blatiner, et al., University of Basle, Basle, Switzerland.

Jeanne, K. M., and M. A. Molot, 1988, *State Capitalism: Public Enterprise in Canada,* Cornell University Press, Ithaca, New York.

Jensen, M. C., 1972, *Studies in the Theory of Capital Markets,* Praeger, New York.

Jhabwala, F., 1973, "A Model of Motivation in State Enterprises in Underdeveloped Economies," *Indian Economic Reviews,* Vol. 8, No. 2, pp. 172-185.

Johansen, L., 1965, *Public Economics,* North Holland Publishing Company, Amsterdam.

Jones, L. P., 1975, *Public Enterprise and Economic Development: The Korean Case,* Korean Development Institute, Seoul, Korea.

_____ ed., 1982, *Public Enterprise in Less Developed Countries,* Cambridge University Press, Cambridge, Massachusetts.

Joskow, P. L., 1976, "Contribution to the Theory of Marginal Cost Pricing," *Bell Journal of Economics,* Vol. 7, No. 1, pp. 197-206.

Kahn, A. E., 1970, *The Economics of Regulation: Principles and Institutions,* John Wiley and Sons, New York.

Kaldor, N., 1980, "Public or Private Enterprise—The Issues to be Considered," in *Public and Private Enterprise in a Mixed Economy;* edited by W. J. Baumol, St. Martin's Press, New York.

Kalecki, M., 1969, *Theory of Economic Dynamics: An Essay on Cyclical and Long-Run Changes in Capitalist Economy*, Augustus Kelly, London.

Kay, J. A., and D. J. Thompson, 1986, "Privatization: A Policy in Search of a Rationale," *Economic Journal*, Vol. 96, No. 381, pp. 18-32.

Kendall, W., 1972, "Labor Relations," in *The State as Entrepreneur: New Dimensions for Public Enterprise;* edited by S. Holland, International Arts and Sciences Press, Inc., New York.

Kessler, F., 1978, *Wall Street Journal*, June 13.

Keyser, W., R. Windle, and R. Stares, 1978, *State Business: Public Enterprise in the EEC*, Metra Oxford Consulting, Oxford, England.

Kim, K. S., 1981, "Enterprise Performance in the Public and Private Sectors: Tanzanian Experience 1970-75," *Journal of Development Areas*, Vol. 15, No. 3, pp. 471-484.

Kornai, J., 1971, *Anti-Equilibrium*, North Holland Publishing Company, Amsterdam.

______ 1982, *Growth, Shortage and Efficiency*, University of California Press, Berkeley.

Kotz, D. M., 1982, "Monopoly, Inflation and Economic Crisis," *Review of Radical Political Economics*, Vol. 14, No. 4, pp. 1-17.

Krapels, N. E., 1977, "Controlling Oil," British Oil Policy and British National Oil Committee on Energy and National Resources, England.

Lange, O., and F. M. Taylor, 1938, *Economic Theory of Socialism*, University of Minnesota Press, Minneapolis.

Lee, F. S., 1984, "Full Cost Prices, Classical Price Theory, and Long Run Period Method of Analysis: A Critical Evaluation," Mimeo, No. 75, April, Department of Economics, University of California, Riverside.

LeGrand, J., and R. Robinson, ed., 1984, *Privatization and the Welfare State*, Allen and Unwin, London, England.

Leibenstein, H., 1966, "Allocative Efficiency vs. X-Efficiency," *American Economic Review*, Vol. 56, No. 3, pp. 392-415.

______ 1978, *General X-efficiency Theory and Economic Development*, Oxford University Press, London.

Lerner, A. P., 1944, *The Economics of Control*, Macmillan Press, New York.

Levine, D. P., 1981, *Economic Theory: The System of Economic Relations as a Whole*, Routledge and Kegan, London, England.

Lewis, W. A., 1952, "The Price Policy of Public Corporations," in *Problems of Nationalized Industries;* edited by W. A. Robson, Oxford University Press, London, England.

Lieberman, S., 1977, *The Growth of European Mixed Economics 1945-1970*, John Wiley and Sons, New York.

Likierman, A., 1984, "The Use of Profitability in Assessing the Performance of Public Enterprises," in *The Public Enterprise in Developing Countries*, edited by V. V. Ramanadham, Croom Helm, Kent, England.

Lindsay, C. M., 1976, "A Theory of Government Enterprise," *Journal of Political Economy*, Vol. 84, No. 5, pp. 1061-1077.

Lintner, J., 1981, "The Economic Theory and Financial Management," in *State-Owned Enterprises in the Western Economies;* edited by R. Vernon and Y. Aharoni, St. Martin's Press, New York.

Lipton, M., 1976, "What is Nationalization For?" *Lloyds Bank Review*, No. 122, July, pp. 33-38.

Little, I.M.D., 1957, *Critique of Welfare Economics*, Oxford University Press, Oxford, England.

Lumby, S., 1981, "New Ways of Financing Nationalized Industries," *Lloyds Bank Review*, No. 141, July, pp. 34-44.

MacAvoy, P. W., W. T. Stanbury, G. Yarrow, and R. J. Zeckhauser, 1989, *Privatization and State-Owned Enterprises*, Kluwer Academic Publishers, Boston.

Marglin, S. A., 1963, "The Social Rate of Discount and the Optimum Rate of Investment," *Quarterly Journal of Economics*, Vol. 77, No. 1, pp. 95-111

Marino, A. M., 1981, "Optimal Departures from Marginal Cost Pricing: The Case of a Rate of Return Constraint," *Southern Economic Journal*, Vol. 48, No. 1, pp. 37-49.

Martinelli, A., 1981, "The Italian Experience: A Historical Perspective," in *State-Owned Enterprise in the Western Economies;* edited by R. Vernon and Y. Aharoni, St. Martin's Press, New York.

Masse, P., 1962, *Optimal Investment Decisions*, Prentice Hall, Englewood Cliffs, New York.

Maunder, P., ed., 1982, *Case Studies in Public Sector Economics*, Heinemann Educational Books, London, England.

McKie, J. W., 1976, "Time's Arrow and Marginal Cost Pricing," in New Dimensions in Public Utility Pricing; edited by H. M. Trebing, Michigan State University, East Lansing.

Meade, J. E., 1944, "Price and Output Policy of State Enterprises," *Economic Journal*, Vol. 54, No. 215, pp. 321-328.

Melody, W. H., 1976, "Comment," in *New Dimensions in Public Utility Pricing;* edited by H. M. Trebing, Michigan State University, East Lansing.

Michalet, C. A., 1974, "France," in *Big Business and the State;* edited by R. Vernon, Harvard University Press, Cambridge, Massachusetts.

Mill, J. S., 1923, *Principles of Political Economy*, Longmans Green Company, London.

Millward, R., 1982, "The Comparative Performance of Public and Private Ownership," in *The Mixed Economy;* edited by E. Roll, Holmes and Meier Publishers, New York.

Ministry of Industry, 1982, The Net Costs of Government Support to Swedish Industry, Allmänna Förlaget, Stockholm.

Mitchell, B. M., and P. R. Kleindorfer, 1979, *Regulated Industries and Public Enterprises*, Lexington Books, Lexington, Massachusetts.

______ W. G. Manning, Jr., and J. P. Acton, 1978, *Peak Load Pricing*, Ballinger Publishing Company, Cambridge, Massachusetts.

Molyneux, R., and D. Thompson, 1987, "Nationalised Industry Performance: Still Third-Rate?" *Fiscal Studies*, Vol. 8, No. 1, pp. 48-82.

Munby, D. L., 1959, "Investing in Coal," *Oxford Economic Papers*, Vol. 11, No. 3, pp. 242-269.

Musgrave, R. A., and P. B. Musgrave, 1989, *Public Finance in Theory and Practice*, McGraw-Hill Book Company, New York.

Musolf, L., 1968, "Public Enterprise in National Development," in *Organization and Administration of Public Enterprises;* edited by A. Hanson, United Nations, New York.

Myers, S. C., 1968, "A Time-State Preference Model of Security Valuation," *Journal of Financial and Quantitative Analysis*, Vol. 3, No. 1, pp. 1-33.

Nadiri, I. M., 1982, "Producer Theory," in *Handbook of Mathematical Economics;* edited by K. J. Arrow and M. D. Intriligator, North Holland Publishing Company, Amsterdam.

National Economics Development Office, 1976, *A Study of U.K. Nationalized Industries*, Appendix B, Her Majesty's Stationery Office, London, England.

Neild, R. R., 1964, "Replacement Policy," National Institute of Economics, *Economic Review*, No. 30, pp. 30-43.

Neilsen, R. P., 1982, "Government-Owned Businesses: Market Presence, Competitive Advantages and Rationales for Their Support by the State," *American Journal of Economics and Sociology*, Vol. 14, No. 1, pp. 17-27.

Nelson, J. R., 1976, "Public Enterprise: Pricing and Investment," in *Public Enterprise, Economic Analysis of Theory and Practice;* edited by W. G. Shepherd, Lexington Books, Lexington, Massachusetts.

Noreng, O., 1981, "State-Owned Oil Companies: Western Europe," in *State-Owned Enterprise in the Western Economies;* edited by R. Vernon and Y. Aharoni, St. Martin's Press, New York.

Norris, H., 1947, "State Enterprise and Output Policy and the Problem of Cost Impution," *Economica*, New Series, Vol. 14, No. 53, pp. 54-62.

Nove, A., 1973, *Efficiency Criteria for Nationalized Industries*, Allen and Unwin, London.

Nugent, J. B., 1973, "A Balance Growth Version of the Linkage Hypothesis," *Quarterly Journal of Economics*, Vol. 87, No. 2, pp. 157-171.

Nunnenkamp, P., 1981, "The Efficiency of State-Owned Enterprises in Manufacturing Industry of Taiwan," *Academic Economic Papers*, Vol. 9, No. 2, pp. 259-276.

Nutter, G. W., 1978, *Growth of Government in the West*, American Enterprise Institute, Washington, D.C.

Okun, A. M., 1981, *Prices and Quantities: Macro Economic Analysis*, Brooking Institution, Washington, D.C.

______ and L. Perry, 1978, *Inflation*, Brooking Institute, Washington, D.C.

Organization for Economic Cooperation and Development, 1981, *Definition and Measurement of the Public Sector*, Economic and Statistics Department, Paris.

Panzar, J., and R. Willig, 1975, "Economies of Scale and Economies of Scope in Multi-Output Production," Economic Discussion Paper, No. 33, Bell Labs, Holmdel, New Jersey.

Pasinetti, L. L., 1977, *Lectures on the Theory of Production*, Columbia University Press, New York.

Peltzman, S., 1971, "Pricing in Public and Private Enterprises: Electric Utilities in the United States," *Journal of Law and Economics*, Vol. 14, No. 1, pp. 109-147.

_____ 1989, "The Control and Performance of State-Owned Enterprises: Comment," in *Privatization and State-Owned Enterprises;* edited by P. W. MacAvoy, W. T. Stanbury, G. Yarrow, and R. J. Zeckhauser, Kluwer Academic Publishers, Boston.

Pescatrice, D. R., and J. M. Trapani, 1980, "The Performance and Objectives of Public and Private Utilities Operation in the United States," *Journal of Public Economics*, Vol. 13, No. 2, pp. 259-276.

Peston, M., 1977, "How Should We Treat Risk?" in *Public Expenditure: Allocation Between Competing Ends;* edited by M. Posner, Cambridge University Press, London.

Pfouts, R. W., 1960, *Essays in Economics and Econometrics in Honor of Harold Hotelling*, University of North Carolina Press, Chapel Hill.

Posner, M. V., ed., 1977, *Public Expenditure Allocation Between Competing Ends*, Cambridge University Press, London.

Prodi, R., 1974, "Italy," in *Big Business and the State: Changing Relations in Western Europe;* edited by R. Vernon, Harvard University Press, Cambridge, Massachusetts.

Prke, R., 1980, "Public Enterprise in Practice: The British Experience of Nationalisation During the Past Decade," in *Public and Private Enterprise in a Mixed Economy;* edited by W. J. Baumol, St. Martin's Press, New York.

_____ 1981, *The Nationalized Industries: Policies and Performance Since 1968*, Martin Robertson, Oxford, England.

Pryor, F. L., 1973, *Property and Industrial Organization in Communist and Capitalist Nations*, Indiana University Press, Bloomington.

Raiffa, H., 1981, "Decision Making in the State-Owned Enterprise," in *State-Owned Enterprise in the Western Economies;* edited by R. Vernon and Y. Aharoni, St. Martin's Press, New York.

Ramamurti, R., 1987, *State-Owned Enterprises: Studies in India and Brazil*, Praeger, New York.

Ramanadham, V. V., 1959, *Problems of Public Enterprise*, Quadrangle Books, Chicago.

Rasamussen, P. N., 1956, *Studies in International Relations*, North Holland Publishing Company, Amsterdam.

Reddy, R. G., 1983, *Government and Public Enterprise*, Frank Cass Tripathi, Bombay, India.

Redwood, J., 1976, "The Future of Nationalized Industries," *Lloyds Bank Review*, No. 123, October, pp. 33-44.

_____ 1976, "Government and the Nationalized Industries," *Lloyds Bank Review*, No. 121, April, pp. 33-46.

_____ 1980, *Public Enterprise in Crisis: The Future of Nationalized Industries*, Basil Blackwell, Oxford, England.

_____ and J. Hatch, 1982, *Controlling Public Industries*, Basil Blackwell, Oxford, England.

Reed, P. W., 1973, *The Economics of Public Enterprise*, Cox and Wyman, London, England.

Rees, R., 1968, "Second Best Rules for Public Enterprise Pricing," *Economica*, New Series, Vol. 35, No. 139, pp. 260-273.

______ 1976, *Public Enterprise Economics*, Weidenfeld and Nicolson, London, England.

Roncaglia, A., 1980, "Production Prices and the Theory of the Firm: A Comment," *Journal of Post Keynesian Economics*, Vol. 3, No. 1, pp. 100-104.

Royal Norwegian Ministry of Finance, 1983, "The Revised National Budget of Norway, 1983," Report No. 88, Oslo, Norway.

Rubenstein, M. E., 1973, "A Mean-Variance Synthesis of Corporate Financial Theory," *Journal of Finance*, Vol. 28, No. 1, pp. 167-182.

Ruggles, N., 1968, "Recent Developments in the Theory of Marginal Cost Pricing," in *Public Enterprises: Selected Readings*; edited by R. Turvey, Penguin Books, Middlesex, England.

Samuels, W. J., 1966, *The Classical Theory of Economic Policy*, The World Publishing Company, New York.

______ and N. Mercuro, 1976, "Property Rights, Equity and Public Utility Pricing," in *New Dimensions in Public Utility Pricing*; edited by H. M. Trebing, Michigan State University, East Lansing.

Samuelson, P., 1948, *Foundations of Economic Analysis*, Harvard University Press, Cambridge, Massachusetts.

______ 1964, "Principles of Efficiency Discussion," *American Economic Review*, Papers and Proceedings, Vol. 54, No. 3, pp. 93-96.

Savas, E. S., 1980, "Comparative Costs of Public and Private Enterprise in Municipal Services," in *Public and Private Enterprise in a Mixed Economy*; edited by W. J. Baumol, St. Martin's Press, New York.

Schefold, B., 1983, "Kahn on Malinvaud," in *Keynes's Economics and the Theory of Value and Distribution*; edited by J. Eatwell and M. Milgate, Duckworth, London.

Schwartz, E., 1970, "The Cost of Capital and Investment Criteria in the Public Sector," *Journal of Finance*, Vol. 25, No. 1, pp. 135-142.

Semmler, W., 1980, "Crisis and Supply-Side Economics: Notes on Recent Changes of the Policy in the U.S.," Mimeo, Department of Economics, New School for Social Research, New York.

______ 1982, "Private Production and the Public Sector," Mimeo, Department of Economics, New School for Social Research, New York.

______ 1983, "On the Classical Theory of Taxation: An Analysis of Tax Incidence in a Linear Production Model," Mimeo, Department of Economics, New School for Social Research, New York.

______ 1984, *Competition, Monopoly, and Differential Profit Rates*, Columbia University Press, New York.

______ 1985, On Technical Changes, Transit Surplus Profit, and Multiple Technique, *Cahiers. D Economie Politique*, No. 10-11, pp. 258-278.

Sheahan, J. B., 1976a, "Experience with Public Enterprise in France and Italy," in Public Enterprise: Economic Analysis of Theory and Practice; edited by W. Shepherd, Lexington Books, Lexington, Massachusetts.

______ 1976b, "Public Enterprise in Developing Countries," in *Public Enterprise: Economic Analysis of Theory and Practice;* edited by W. Shepherd, Lexington Books, Lexington, Massachusetts.

Shepherd, W., 1965, *Economic Performance Under Public Ownership,* Yale University Press, New Haven, Connecticut.

______ 1976a, "Price Structure, Social Efficiency and Equity," in *New Dimensions in Public Utility Pricing;* edited by H. M. Trebing, Michigan State University, East Lansing.

______ 1976b, *Public Enterprise: Economic Analysis of Theory and Practice,* Lexington Books, Lexington, Massachusetts.

Shirley, M. M., 1983, *Managing State-Owned Enterprises,* World Bank Staff Working Paper No. 577, Washington, D.C.

Shonfield, A., 1982, *The Use of Public Power,* Oxford University Press, London.

Short, R. P., 1983, "The Role of Public Enterprises: An International Statistical Comparison," International Monetary Fund, Washington, D.C.

Skandinaviska, Enskilda Banken, 1983, "Some Data About Sweden 1983-1984," Skandinaviska, Enskilda Banken, New York.

Smith, A., 1937, *Wealth of Nations,* Modern Library, New York.

Smith, A. D., D.M.W.N. Hitchens, and S. W. Davies, 1982, *International Industrial Productivity: A Comparison of Britain, America, and Germany,* Press Syndicate of University of Cambridge, Cambridge, England.

Smith, G. P., 1979, "*The Test Discount Rate,*" Working Paper No. 9, Her Majesty's Stationery Office, London, England.

Stapleton, R. C., and M. G. Subrahmanyam, 1978, "Capital Market Equilibrium a Mixed Economy, Optimal Public Sector Investment Decision Rules and the Social Rate of Discount," *Quarterly Journal of Economics,* Vol. 92, No. 3, pp. 399-411.

Steel, W. F., and J. W. Evans, 1984, *Industrialization in Sub-Saharan Africa: Strategies and Performance,* World Bank, Washington, D.C.

Stigler, G., 1976, "The Existence of X-Efficiency," *American Economic Review,* Vol. 66, No. 1, pp. 213-216.

Thurow, L. C., 1983, *Dangerous Currents: The State of Economics,* Random House, Inc., New York.

Tivey, L. J., ed., 1973, *Nationalized Industries Since 1960: A Book of Reading,* Allen and Unwin, London.

Tool, M. R., 1979, *The Discretionary Economy,* Goodyear Publishing Company, Santa Monica, California.

Treasury, 1946, *Coal Industry Nationalization Act,* Her Majesty's Stationery Office, London, England.

______ 1956, *Report of the Committee of Inquiry into the Electricity Supply Industry,* Cmnd 9672, Her Majesty's Stationery Office, London, England.

_____ 1967, *Nationalized Industries: A Review of Economic and Financial Objectives*, Cmnd 3437, Her Majesty's Stationery Office, London, England.

_____ 1976, *Steel Nationalization*, Cmnd 2651, Her Majesty's Stationery Office, London, England.

_____ 1978a, *The Nationalized Industries*, Cmnd 7131, Her Majesty's Stationery Office, London, England.

_____ 1978b, *The Test Discount Rate and the Required Rate of Return*, Proceedings of Seminar held at the Civil Service College, June 16-17, Sunningdale, England.

Trebing, H. M., ed., 1976, *New Dimensions in Public Utility Pricing*, Michigan State University, East Lansing.

Trivedi, P., 1985, Performance Evaluation and Explanation of Public and Private Behavior: Issues, Methodology and the Case of Indian Cement Industry, Unpublished Ph.D. Thesis, Boston University, Boston, Massachusetts.

Turvey, R., 1971, *Economics Analysis and Public Enterprises*, Allen and Unwin, London.

_____ ed., 1968, *Public Enterprise: Selected Readings*, Penguin Books, Middlesex, England.

United Nations, 1954, Some Problems in the Organization and Administration of Public Enterprises in the Industrial Field, United Nations, New York.

_____ 1968, A System of National Income Accounts, United Nations, New York.

_____ 1976, Finance of Public Enterprise in Developing Countries: Coordination, Forms and Sources, United Nations Department of Economic and Social Affairs, New York.

Varian, H. R., 1978, *Microeconomic Analysis*, W. W. Norton and Company, Inc., New York.

Venkata, G. C., and D. Dakshinamurthy, 1986, "Performance of Public Enterprises in India: Impact of Heavy External Finance," *Public Enterprise*, Vol. 6, No. 2, pp. 147-155.

Vernon, R., 1974, "Enterprise and Government in Western Europe," in *Big Business and State;* edited by R. Vernon, Harvard University Press, Cambridge, Massachusetts.

_____ and Y. Aharoni, ed., 1981, *State-Owned Enterprise in the Western Economies*, St. Martin's Press, New York.

Vickers, J. and G. Yarrow, 1988, *Privatization: An Economic Analysis*, MIT Press, Cambridge, Massachusetts.

Vickrey, W., 1948, "Some Objections to Marginal Cost Pricing," *Journal of Political Economy*, Vol. 56, No. 1, pp. 218-238

_____ 1964, "Principles of Efficiency Discussion," *American Economic Review*, Proceedings, Vol. 54, No. 3, pp. 88-92.

_____ 1983, "Marginal Cost Pricing: Using the Short Run for the Long Run," paper presented at the 9th Annual Convention in Eastern Economic Association, Boston, Massachusetts.

Walker, A., ed., 1982, *Public Expenditure and Social Policy*, Heinemann Educational Books, London.

Walstedt, B., 1980, *State Manufacturing Enterprise in a Mixed Economy: The Turkey Case*, Johns Hopkins University Press, Baltimore, Maryland.

Webb, M. G., 1973, *The Economics of Nationalized Industries: A Theoretical Approach*, Nelson and Sons, London.

_____ 1976a, "A Critical Appraisal for U.K. Policy for Nationalized Industries," in *Regulated Industries and Public Enterprises;* edited by B. M. Mitchell and P. R. Kleindorfer, Lexington Books, Lexington, Massachusetts.

_____ 1976b, *Pricing Policies for Public Enterprise*, Macmillan Press, London.

_____ 1979, *Economic Analysis*, Sevenoake, Butterworth, England.

Weisbrod, B. A., 1988, *The Nonprofit Economy*, Harvard University Press, Cambridge, Massachusetts.

White, L. J., 1976, "Appropriate Technology, X-inefficiency and a Competitive Environment: Some Evidence from Pakistan," *Quarterly Journal of Economics*, Vol. 90, No. 4, pp. 575-589.

Wickham, S., 1969, "Management and Financial Constraints in Public Enterprise," in *Public Economics;* edited by J. Margolis and H. Gutton, Macmillan Press, London.

Wilson, T., 1945, "Price and Output Policy of State Enterprise," *Economic Journal*, Vol. 55, No. 220, pp. 454-461.

World Bank, 1980, *Borrowing in International Capital Markets*, World Bank, Washington, D.C.

_____ 1983, *World Development Report 1983*, Oxford University Press, New York.

Yunker, J. A., 1975, "Economic Performance of Public and Private Enterprise: The Case of U.S. Electric Utilities," *Journal of Economics and Business*, Vol. 28, No. 1, pp. 60-67.

Author Index

Subject Index

For Product Safety Concerns and Information please contact our EU representative GPSR@taylorandfrancis.com Taylor & Francis Verlag GmbH, Kaufingerstraße 24, 80331 München, Germany

Batch number: 10726013

Printed by Printforce, the Netherlands